Dissent in the Years of Khrushchev

Also by Erik Kulavig

MECHANISMS OF POWER IN THE SOVIET UNION (*editor*)

SOVIET CIVILIZATION BETWEEN PAST AND PRESENT (*editor*)

RUSSIAN NATIONALISM, 1986–92

PROPAGANDA AND EVERYDAY LIFE IN RUSSIA, 1924–36

Dissent in the Years of Khrushchev

Nine Stories about Disobedient Russians

Erik Kulavig

palgrave
macmillan

First published 2002 by
PALGRAVE MACMILLAN
Houndmills, Basingstoke, Hampshire RG21 6XS and
175 Fifth Avenue, New York, N.Y. 10010
Companies and representatives throughout the world

PALGRAVE MACMILLAN is the global academic imprint of the Palgrave
Macmillan division of St. Martin's Press LLC and of Palgrave Macmillan Ltd.
Macmillan® is a registered trademark in the United States, United Kingdom
and other countries. Palgrave is a registered trademark in the European
Union and other countries.

ISBN 0-333-99037-4

This book is printed on paper suitable for recycling and
made from fully managed and sustained forest sources.

A catalogue record for this book is available
from the British Library.

Library of Congress Cataloging-in-Publication Data

Kulavig, Erik.
    Dissent in the years of Khrushchev: nine stories about disobedient
    Russians / Erik Kulavig.
        p. cm
    Includes bibliographical references and index.
    ISBN 0-333-99037-4 (cloth)
    1. Soviet Union – History – 1953–1985. 2. Government, Resistance to –
Soviet Union. I. Title.

DK274 .K828 2002
947.085–dc21

                                                                2002022417

10 9 8 7 6 5 4 3 2 1
11 10 09 08 07 06 05 04 03 02

Printed and bound in Great Britain by
Antony Rowe Ltd, Chippenham and Eastbourne

To Pia, Thea and Mads

Contents

Foreword

Thanks are due to the Danish Research Council, the Danish Foreign Policy Institute (DUPI), and the University of Southern Denmark for financial support, and thanks to the kind people at the Central Party Archive (TsKhSD) in Moscow, the Hoover archives at Stanford University, and the Hoover Institution on Revolution, War and Peace.

I am grateful for the comments made by my university colleagues and the members of the research network: Continuity and Change in Russia, the Baltic States and Eastern Europe. Special thanks go to Professor Arfon Rees at EUI for useful criticism and encouragement.

Erik Kulavig

Introduction

Stalinism is ... 'a Marxism that depends on holding together
by brutal force an economy that would otherwise disintegrate
for lack of popular consent.'

Robert Conquest in *Russia after Khrushchev*

One of the most unmanageable myths about Russian history and about
the Russian national character is that Russians always submit themselves to the authority of a strong leader no matter how cruel and
unfair his regime. It is not the aim of this book to deny the existence of
such a mentality, but rather to argue for the fact that it was always at
least accompanied by its opposite, ranging from open rebellion to
more quiet forms of everyday resistance and disobedience to the rulers
and the system. The focus of the book is on the Soviet period, and
more specifically on the Khrushchev years.

Popular resistance to the Communist regime was expressed most
concretely during the process of forced collectivization, which issued
in virtual civil war. But there were other instances of confrontation
between state and society, including uprisings in the numerous forced
labour camps, before, during and after Stalin's rule. The Party's
control over society, and the general suppression of the population,
which reached their height under Stalin but never completely disappeared from the Soviet system, meant, certainly, that resistance was
expressed for the most part tacitly and passively. In some respects,
however, this form of everyday resistance posed a greater problem to
the authorities than open opposition, precisely because it was mostly
concealed and therefore much harder to detect and stamp out. The
low level of productivity in the state sector and the *kolkhozes* (collective farms) could in this sense be seen as one of the most widespread

1

forms of passive resistance. Such resistance was characteristic of the entire Stalin period, but became especially pronounced towards the end of his rule. It was this form of resistance that Khrushchev's reforms especially targeted. He realized that unless the Party went some way to meeting the population's demands for food, housing, consumer goods and personal security, productivity would never reach a satisfactory level, and what remained of the Party's legitimacy would disappear.

Although we should be careful not to exaggerate, there is no doubt that Khrushchev's reforms brought the population certain material and – more particularly – political benefits. Nevertheless, the reforms failed to live up to expectations – which, it should be noted, were encouraged through Party propaganda. The population thus continued to manifest widespread disobedience in key areas within the social and economic life of the country. Neither Khrushchev nor any of his successors was able to win the people's confidence in the Party and the state and thereby cause the 'socialist machine' to deliver effectively. Moreover, the substantial reduction in political terror, which was perhaps Khrushchev's most significant achievement, meant that the population, no longer so cowed, became gradually bolder in expressing dissatisfaction.

The present study, which focuses on reactions to the political leadership among the Russian population, indicates that social unrest and (mainly) disobedience in the communist regimes following Stalin's death, and especially after the 20th Party Congress in 1956, was not confined to Poland and Hungary, but struck root in a similar way at the very core of the Communist empire – in the Soviet Union itself. Moreover it is argued that reasons for the final collapse of the Soviet Union in 1991 should be looked for in this field.

Before we enter the history of society of the Khrushchev era we will briefly discuss what was going on in the sphere of high politics in those years, and then consider the overall point of view of this study.

The historical context

There is general agreement that there were considerable differences between the manner in which Stalin and Khrushchev respectively ruled the country. Stalin's rule was predominantly based on brutal suppression and fear, whereas Khrushchev attempted to co-operate with society. Gorbachev was the most direct heir to Khurschev's model, but his predecessor, Brezhnev, albeit with a certain reluctance, also tended more to this form of leadership than to the Stalinist style.

Notwithstanding the differences between these models, however, the underlying similarities were so fundamental that one cannot speak of any genuine reform of the Soviet system until after 1991.[1] Like Stalin, Khrushchev and Brezhnev could not accept the existence of either a political or an economic market. There could be no ownership of the means of production, no consumer power, no multi-party system, no autonomous concentration of political or economic might, nor any acceptance of the public space as a market place for ideas. Although Gorbachev during the last years of his regime came close to a radical break with this all-embracing model, he nevertheless clung to socialism's basic tenets concerning state ownership of land and the means of production.

In the early 1930s the following monologue could be heard in Soviet theatres:

'... 80 percent of all those questioned live in constant fear. The dairyman is afraid that his cow will be confiscated, the farmer is afraid of forced collectivisation, the civil servant of the constant purges, the Party functionary is afraid of being caught in making concessions, the scientist of accusations of idealism, the technician is afraid of being accused of sabotage. We live in the epoch of great fear. Fear makes talented researchers deny their own methods and cheat about their social origins ... .

Fear dogs a person's heels ... . A person becomes untrustworthy, reserved, unreliable, careless and unprincipled ... . Fear gives rise to absenteeism, delayed trains, disrupted production, poverty and hunger. No one does anything without being ordered to, without the threat of being publicly shamed, or of being dismissed or put in prison. A rabbit, which catches sight of a snake, is unable to move out of the way, its muscles are petrified, and it waits obediently for the snake's muscles to contract and suffocate it. We are all rabbits. Can we possibly work creatively after this? Of course we can't. Get rid of the fear, get rid of everything that creates fear, and then you will see our land bloom!'

These words are taken from the play *Strakh (Fear)* of 1931 by the dramatist Afinogenov and express very accurately the dilemma of totalitarianism.[2] Control, violence and suppression were so all-embracing that society was brought to the brink of paralysis. Afinogenov was not a critic of the system but a true servant of it, and he was upset, for good reason, that the public reacted most strongly to the scene described above, rather than to the ovation on the system, which he had intended as the highpoint of the play.

The fear, which grew in the 1930s, diminished in various ways during the Second World War and expectations were engendered of better times once the trials of the war were overcome. However, the good times were long in coming, and when the Party regained control and fully returned to suppression as a means of government, society reacted with falling productivity and apathy and in some cases even with open resistance. One legacy of Stalin's rule was thus an oppressed and resentful population whose attitude to Party rule was grudging and hostile.

Following Stalin's death at the beginning of March 1953 a power struggle arose amongst his closest colleagues, which was not finally resolved until July 1957. By this time Khrushchev had used his considerable political skills to secure his control over both Party and state. Significantly, the chief rivals in the power struggle ended up virtually competing to distinguish themselves as reformers by distancing themselves from Stalin's methods of leadership. It was paradoxical, but hardly accidental, that Beria, who as head of Stalin's secret police had been responsible for the apparatus of mass repression, himself led the struggle with a series of reform initiatives. There appears thus to have been a clear understanding that if the Soviet system were to survive, the leadership needed to regain the confidence of Soviet society.

On 24 March 1953 Beria presented to the Party leadership a proposal for a far-reaching amnesty for the nearly 2.5 million prisoners held in the notorious forced labour camps.[3] The result was that approximately one million prisoners were released. Beria moreover played a key role in exposing the so-called doctors' plot, which in January 1953 had led to the arrest of a number of doctors connected with the Kremlin, and which was widely seen as the start of a new purge. Beria also proposed that the peasants should be given the right to cultivate more land for private use, and that collectivization should be brought to a halt in those areas annexed after the Second World War, that is, the Western Ukraine and the Baltic states. Finally, with regard to the crisis in the German Democratic Republic (DDR) in 1953, the result of a growing division between the country's political leadership and its population, Beria proposed that the Socialist Unity Party, led by Walter Ulbricht, should work towards the reunification of a democratic Germany. In this connection the East German leadership should halt its attempts to impose socialism forcibly, and in particular abolish collectivization, which had met with strong resistance among German farmers.

By virtue of his position as the leader of the secret police, with its extensive network of agents and informants, Beria was probably better informed than anyone else in the Soviet Union about the state of public opinion and was therefore, perhaps, the person best placed to see where and how the leadership could intervene to prevent the conflicts which potentially threatened the system. It is not accidental, therefore, that several of Beria's ideas were later adopted by Khrushchev – though not before he got rid of him in a manner which had more in common with Stalinist practices than with the new epoch he had otherwise ushered in. Fear and hatred of Beria led the rest of the Party leadership to turn against him, and he was executed in December 1953. Khrushchev appears to have been the prime instigator behind this move, in which he showed considerable personal courage and drive.

With the execution of Beria, Khrushchev had got rid of the strongest link in the *troika* which had established itself as the country's collective leadership even as Stalin lay on his deathbed, and which consisted, apart from Beria, of Malenkov and Molotov. Malenkov was the Prime Minister; Beria the leader of the newly-fused Ministry of Internal Affairs (MVD) and Ministry of Security (MGB); and Molotov the Foreign Minister.

Malenkov was the first to come forward with a programme which demanded a relatively major shift in priorities, principally away from the defence industry, and which favoured a long-term strategy for improving the population's material conditions, with economic incentives replacing Party campaigns in the effort to boost productivity. For obvious reasons this programme was opposed by the defence industry and the army, as well as by those among the political leadership who considered it essential to bring about a more rapid improvement in living standards. Khrushchev responded with a programme that offered a short-term solution to the problem of material provisions, at what appeared to be minimal cost to the military industrial complex and to the Party's mobilizing role in the economy. His simple solution was to propose a national campaign to promote the cultivation of hitherto uncultivated land in the east. This would relatively quickly put bread on the table, and the size of the investments involved would not entail reducing the defence budget to nearly the same extent as proposed by Malenkov.

Khruschchev was convinced that it was possible in the short term to make the existing agricultural system more efficient by introducing new crops and new methods of cultivation, by improving management and leadership and, not least, by raising state purchase prices. Local heads of agricultural organizations came under constant attack for relying far too heavily on central funds rather than on improving and increasing local production. He believed that with proper leadership even the weakest *kolkhoz* could be brought up to the same level as the best, and he even offered personally to go out in the fields and do what needed to be done. Investment should not come directly from the state, but indirectly through higher purchase prices, which would give a greater incentive to produce. The state should then ensure, through its campaigns, that the increased profits would not simply be consumed but be reinvested in agriculture.

Khrushchev consciously played on the anxiety among both local leaders and the rest of the elite about popular dissatisfaction with the provision of goods, and this was no doubt why his political programme for a quick solution won widespread support and added to his strength politically. At the same time, however, he made himself extremely dependent on the capacity and willingness of the agricultural sector to redeem his repeated and ever-more-radical promises of better production results. As early as July 1954, for example, he declared that by 1970 the Soviet Union would be in a position to provide its citizens with a better standard of living than the USA. Statements of this kind created a pressure of expectation not just among the political elite, but also among the population at large. Khrushchev's political life and, in the longer term, the survival of the regime itself became dependent on whether or not the agricultural sector would begin to deliver. The gravity of the situation was underlined in a speech at a plenary meeting of the Central Committee in autumn 1953, when Khrushchev reported not merely that there was a huge gap between supply and demand in agricultural produce, but that this was creating a serious political problem:

> Whereas Soviet citizens were previously willing to make do with ordinary bread, there are growing demands now for more and better. There is an increasing demand for sugar, fruit, berries and grapes. Whereas the population used previously to limit their consumption of animal products, they are now demanding more meat, butter, milk and eggs.[4]

Principally thanks to the cultivation of new areas in the East (the Virgin Lands), there was a significant improvement in production results in the period from 1953 to 1958. To a lesser extent there was also an increase in productivity, but the overall level still fell far short of that in the USA and Western Europe. In so far as productivity improved, this was due to the increase in state purchase prices, to the introduction of a minimum wage for *kolkhoz* workers and to other incentives which made it economically worth while for individual peasants to put greater effort into cultivating *kolkhoz* land.

In 1960, it became clearly apparent for the first time that Khrushchev's reform programme was nowhere near being able to meet the high

expectations his regime had encouraged. Production in the newly cultivated territories in the East had been catastrophic the previous year, and
indeed would never live up to expectations. State purchase prices for agricultural products had steadily increased throughout the period, but were
never sufficient to cover production costs, which hardly encouraged the
collective farmers to produce and sell their produce to the state. There
was far too little surplus to invest in new machinery or buildings. The
campaigns and the political pressure to fulfil the plans led local Party
people to commandeer seed corn and animals from the *kolkhoz* peasants'
private plots. These repeated attacks on the private sector in turn led the
peasants to withhold their private produce from the market.[5]

Stalin's successors were broadly in accord about the need to distance
themselves from what would later, under Gorbachev, be known as the
command economy – the over-centralized management and brutal
control that had dominated the Stalin period – and on the consequent
need to find new forms of administration and control. They agreed
that it was essential to some extent to decentralize the decision-making
process and the responsibility for production results; and to rationalize
planning and scale down the huge planning apparatus. There was,
however, considerable disagreement as to how all this should be imple-
mented. Malenkov was in favour of maintaining the ministerial
system, but wanted to see less pressure put on factory managers and
hence less interference by the Party in the daily management of production. Khrushchev, on the other hand, favoured re-establishing the
Party's leading role in the economy. He believed that it was possible to
decentralize the decision-making process, yet step up the Party's
involvement in the economy by having local Party branches monitor
fulfilment of the plan. Under Stalin the Party had been sidelined in
economic affairs; power had accrued instead to the various ministries
responsible for the different branches of the economy, which the
dictator himself had some difficulty in controlling.[6]

One of Khrushchev's fundamental beliefs was that decisions concerning day-to-day management and planning should be taken as close as
possible to the actual site of production. Hence the fact that from 1954
to 1955 some 11,000 enterprises were shifted from central to local
control, while in 1956 firms that fell under the authority of no fewer
than 12 departmental ministries in the central government were likewise transferred to the local authorities. The process culminated, in
May 1957, in the replacement of most of the departmental ministries
with approximately one hundred economic councils (*sovnarkhozy*).[7] It
was intended that these councils would co-ordinate, on a regional

basis, the activities of different sectors within the economy. This shift to regional planning would, it was hoped, bring two main advantages. First, through their greater proximity to local enterprises the councils would be able to acquire more detailed knowledge of their work, and would thus be in a better position to guide and control them. Second, the new system would be conducive to greater co-operation among the different sectors within each region, which would therefore reap the benefits of a proper division of labour. By contrast, the perpetual bottlenecks within the old, centrally planned system had meant that each sector had aimed to be self-sufficient in as many areas as possible.

The rationale behind this reform was not solely economic. It was also directed against Malenkov and his supporters, who represented the majority in the Party's most powerful organ, the presidium, and whose own political support-base, it should be noted, lay in the traditional hierarchy of the planned economy. The introduction of the economic councils and the abolition of the departmental ministries would remove this power base; hence their vain attempt to get rid of Khrushchev through the formation of the so-called Anti-Party group in 1957. Khrushchev, however, allied himself with the local Party bosses who, through his reforms, would gain greater influence via their control of the local economic councils. This alliance ultimately ensured not only Khrushchev's victory in the battle for power, but also the reinstatement of the Party, as opposed to the government and all its ministries, as the central agent in the planning of the economy.

From an economic point of view it made sense to decentralize the decision-making process and the responsibility for economic results, but it should be emphasized that there was never any intention, via these reforms, to abolish the planned system or the command economy as such. The central features of that system remained in place: decisions were still determined first and foremost by political considerations rather than by a market which could set appropriate prices, indicate to the agents involved where it would be most advantageous to invest, and force them through competition to improve the efficiency of their production and the quality of their products. Khrushchev thus inherited the central weakness of the Stalin model, namely that it made more sense for economic agents to claim that they had fulfilled or over-fulfilled the plan, than actually to produce efficiently.

The centralized version of the planned economy had demonstrated that it was a great deal less efficient than the market economy, and this proved no less true of Khrushchev's decentralized version. As already mentioned, political decision-makers retained their primacy in the economic realm: in place of rational economic calculations based on market-driven prices, the new regime could offer only the numerous campaigns of the Khrushchev era, which did nothing to solve the key problems of information and control which had dogged the traditional model. These problems were manifest, for example, in the decisions made by certain local party bosses to slaughter valuable breeding cattle in order to fulfil the plans for meat deliveries, regardless of the long-term economic effects or of what was economically rational for society as a whole.

There was a further weakness in the new system, which was a direct result of the decentralization brought about by introducing the economic councils. One of the main economic arguments for abolishing the departmental ministries had been to put a stop to the 'empire building' which had split the economy into numerous semi-autonomous empires, severely limiting communication and co-operation among different sectors and hence jeopardizing the economy as a whole. By forcing the different sectors to co-operate and institute a proper division of labour within each region, the *sovnarkhozy* did indeed solve this problem, but in the process introduced another – one that, from the point of view of the total economy, may indeed have been even more negative in its effects. For the more than a hundred economic regions proved to be every bit as selfish as the former departmental ministries. Their first priority was to promote, by whatever means available, their own regional interests, regardless of whether this benefited the country as a whole. It soon became apparent that local Party leaders felt a greater loyalty towards their region than to the central Party leadership in Moscow. Khrushchev's oft-repeated attacks on and denunciations of local patriotism (*mestnichestvo*) by and large proved fruitless. Moral exhortations and various forms of sanctions could do nothing to remedy the structural forces behind this new form of empire-building – not this time in the abolished ministries, but in the regional councils.

Towards the end of his regime Khrushchev himself admitted that his policy of decentralization had been a mistake, and embarked once more on trying to pull the threads together in Moscow. Thus in July 1964 he proposed that 17 agricultural organizations be set up in Moscow which would be responsible for planning and administering agriculture in the individual republics. This policy met with resistance among Khrushchev's own political support-base, the local Party secretaries, who saw it as an attempt to clip their wings.

The aim of decentralization had been to force the 'socialist machine' to deliver so that the population's 'material and cultural needs' could be satisfied. The core of the whole project was to raise the alarmingly low level of production by boosting productivity. The solution, in Khrushchev's view, lay in putting greater responsibility for production results on local authorities by decentralizing economic control. The policy proved only partially successful, and certainly failed to live up to the promises of the Party leadership and, not least, the expectations of Soviet citizens. Even Khrushchev's reformed version of the planned economy was unable to get rid of the inherent weaknesses of the command model. The socialist experiment of replacing self-interest with collectivist ideals as the driving force in the economy, and substituting political commands and bureaucratic control for the laws of the market, including its price mechanisms, had led to a degree of economic stagnation which threatened the very survival of the regime. Khrushchev's reforms had been directly motivated by this threat, but they did not touch the core of the old system and hence failed to issue in the expected results.

Modernization theory and the Russian under-society

The wave of reform, which gathered momentum after Stalin's death, is often explained as a result of the modernization of the Soviet economy and of Soviet society which had begun under Stalin. In Marxist terms, the forces of production had overtaken the relations of production. Moreover – so the argument goes – the economy had developed to a degree where it could no longer be steered from a single centre; decision-making power thus had to be transferred to local authorities and individual enterprises. At the same time, the population as a whole was now better educated, which in turn led to greater demands for influence and for a higher standard of living.[8] While there is undoubtedly much to be said for this so-called 'modernization theory', there are grounds for scepticism over the claim that Stalin's regime was compatible with the first phase of this modernisation process, and only in its second phase became a barrier to further development. This implicit legitimization of Stalin's methods is not just improper but mistaken. Not only does it ignore the vast waste of human and natural resources, which was a direct result of Stalin's extreme level of mobilization; it also leaves out of account the widespread popular resistance to the regime.

The break-up of the Soviet Union gave rise to something in the nature of a paradigm shift in research on Soviet history. Instead of seeking to explain what held the regime together, researchers began investigating the reasons why it eventually fell apart, and with the gradual opening up of the archives, new interest arose in the social history of the country. As a result, historians began to question the assumption that the Stalinist system had in some sense suited the level of social development in pre-war Soviet society.

In an in-depth analysis of certain large-scale strikes among textile workers in the Ivanovo region in 1932, an American historian demonstrated how enthusiasm for the Soviet system among workers was more the exception than the rule. He maintains that if anyone has been able to argue the contrary, it is either because they have focused on young communists in the cities, who profited from Stalin's revolution from above, or because their access to archive material has been too limited.[9] Another investigation, which lends support to this thesis, shows how ordinary Russians in the period between 1934 and 1941 not only maintained a healthy scepticism towards those in power, but often came into direct opposition with them. The prevailing outlook thus seems to have been one of 'them' versus 'us', that is to say, the Party bureaucracy or the state bureaucracy versus the ordinary citizen: certainly not the view that the Party's agitators had tried to inculcate in the people.[10]

The Russian economic historian A.M. Timofeev has argued that the history of the Soviet Union is not that of the building of a strong state, but, on the contrary, the story of the gradual collapse of state power.[11] His point is that very few Soviet citizens were ever truly persuaded by Communist doctrine or Party propaganda; by far the majority continued, on the contrary, to believe in universal ideas and values in which individual goals and individual happiness took precedence over those of the collective, the society or the state. In this sense they found themselves at odds with state doctrine and the Soviet regime; however, this was rarely expressed in open conflict, but rather in the quiet, everyday practice of resistance, which ultimately undermined the very foundations of the regime. Opposition was manifested most directly in the so-called shadow economy: that sphere of semi-legal or illegal activity to which citizens devoted an ever-increasing part of their time and energy, to the detriment of their contribution to the legal state economy. This 'private economic activity' was frequently conducted within the framework of the state sphere. The director of a state trading enterprise would use his position to conduct private businesses; a state-employed doctor would offer private consultations on the side; and a factory machinist would use part of his paid time to produce items for his own use or for sale and exchange. Timofeev in this sense refers to a 'privatization' of the Soviet economy. There was of course, no private ownership of land or factories in the Soviet Union; instead, the private economy was based on employees' access to state-owned means of production. Soviet workers 'held a piece of property in their hands'. They became, in this sense, the *de facto* owners of the means of production and were able up to a point to use this position to their own advantage. The extent and nature of this private activity naturally depended on the individual's place in the overall hierarchy, but in principle this possibility was open to everyone. Even the severest forms of control were powerless to stamp out this kind of private business. In principle Soviet citizens had available to them the same three options that were open to citizens in a liberal regime:

1. to behave as prescribed by doctrine;
2. partially to do as prescribed;
3. to do the opposite of what was prescribed.

The choice among these options was generally motivated by considerations of personal advantage. Individual profit thus remained, according to Timofeev, the sole genuine motive for economic activity within the Soviet system. In support of this thesis he cites the following statement by the Soviet economist F.S. Varga – who, it should be noted, was himself an orthodox adherent of the system: 'With few exceptions everyone in the Soviet Union strives to increase their own income. This remains the most important goal in the individual's life, just as it is under capitalism.'[12]

The Soviet citizen's 'shadow behaviour' encompassed not just the economy but the whole of everyday life – everything that went on outside, or alongside, the realm of Communist doctrine. In Timofeev's estimation: 'Such contempt for the written law ... nay, such denial of the written law of a state power has never been known elsewhere in history.'[13]

The break-up of the Soviet system can thus be explained as the victory of a living alternative over Soviet doctrine. An uprising on the part of the *de facto* owners of state property provoked the crisis. After the mid-1950s, when Khrushchev's reforms were pushed through and, as Yavlinskii writes, there was no longer a KGB agent stationed behind every lathe, this *de facto* ownership spread ever more widely through the Soviet system.[14] When in the mid-1980s Gorbachev put into effect his package of reforms, economic agents began to transform their *de facto* entitlement into *de jure* ownership. The 1987 law on co-operatives was one of the legal instruments brought into play. In 1991–92, when the shift to capitalism was publicly declared and the official privatization process began, it dawned on the Russian leadership that *de facto* privatization had already taken place and that in reality there was not a great deal of ownerless property to sell off. The shadow economy was not therefore just a secondary side-effect or a fail-safe device in the Soviet economy, serving merely to hold rebellion at bay, but a significant part of the Soviet system, and perhaps the only part to survive the overhaul of 1991. In the mid-1990s a substantial part of the economy was still 'black'. Thus only around half of citizens' earnings were paid through legal channels.

The social-historical framework for understanding Soviet history sketched out above entails shifting our attention away from political doctrine and the role of ideology towards the everyday reality of Soviet life. In investigating how this everyday life functioned, we find that the driving force within it lay in the Soviet 'under-society', and that the motives for action within this society were the classic economic stimuli of self-interest and personal happiness. There is no doubt that the quiet but persistent pressure exerted by this part of society played a major role in the eventual demise of the system in 1991.

Timofeev focuses on the shadow economy, but suggests that it serves only as an illustration of the overall 'shadow culture' in Soviet society, and that elements, or whole systems, of alternative behaviour and consciousness could be found not only in the economy but also in other areas. This proposition in itself may not seem novel; the existence of both religious and political dissidents is well known, and we have long referred to the Soviet system as a 'two-culture' system. What is new is the proposition that this 'second culture', or at least the economic part of it, had a great many more members than the relatively few whom we have traditionally called dissidents.

I am aware of Timofeev's adherence to the belief that the market economy and private ownership are virtual forces of nature, which no culturally constructed barrier can in the end hold back. This of course is debatable; suffice it to say, perhaps, that the 'under-society' had a historical memory of an older economic system which inevitably resurfaced under the new regime.

Note on the sources

The Soviet state kept a watchful eye on citizens and social developments. In addition to the KGB a number of departments under the Central Committee had the task of collecting information on public reaction to Party or government decisions and on both national and international political events. Of course one should be wary of uncritically taking their reports as direct expressions of what was actually happening in society. One can imagine, for instance, that the KGB had an interest in describing events as dramatically as possible with the aim of increasing the organization's own licence to act. But granted this and other reservations, these reports can nevertheless give us more detailed and sometimes new information.

The sources for most of the work are documents from the Committee for Party Control (Komitet Partiinogo Kontrolya or KPK), which was one of the countless sub-organizations serving the Central Committee. This organization was succeeded in 1934 by the Central Control Commission, but the latter's main task was, as before, to keep a check on whether the Party's resolutions were being carried out in practice, and a watch on individual members' behaviour and morals. From 1962 until 1965 the organization was called the Committee for Party and State Control, and even though this name covered its activities more comprehensively – as we know it was in any case impossible to separate Party from state – it reverted in 1965 to its previous title.

An important part of the KPK's tasks, aside from those already mentioned, consisted of investigating appeals from Party members or ordinary citizens who considered themselves to have been unfairly treated by the local authorities or at work, or letters from people who were reporting various violations of Party or government rules and norms. This covered everything from marital break-ups to poor discipline at work, drinking, brawling, disobedience, theft, economic offences and sadistic behaviour by camp commanders, to actual political activities.

The organization commanded a widely branching network of sub-organizations and a large number of inspectors, who were sent out into the field when the central leadership in Moscow wished to get an overview of a particular case. Until 1957 the KPK had plenipotentiaries in the republics and at *krai* (regional) and *oblast* (district) level. The inspectors' task was to carry out a thorough investigation of each case and to issue reports. If considered sufficiently significant, these reports were then forwarded to the Central Committee by the heads of the KPK. The KPK's archive thus contains complaints and appeals by Party members and ordinary citizens, the inspectors' investigations, various kinds of testimony and other documents relating to each case.

The KPK was a Party organization and thus an important brick in the system of Party control and suppression. For the period we are concerned with, however, there appears to have been a quite considerable coincidence of interests between the citizens and the KPK in their struggle against bureaucracy, arbitrariness and other 'left-overs from Stalin's time'. To a certain extent the KPK thus seems to have been caught up on the bandwagon of Khrushchev's reforms. This does not mean that the reports were objective, but they were critical and to a certain extent reflected the attitudes of citizens themselves.

The time-frame for this investigation, 1953–64, more or less corresponds with Nikita Khrushchev's time in power. This period has a number of features in common with the Gorbachev period (1985–91). In both cases the Party sought through reform to revitalize society within the framework of socialism. In the first case, as we know, this process was halted before the power of the Party itself collapsed. In the second instance, it was to all appearances no longer possible to apply the brakes. In both cases the reforms can be explained as the result primarily of indirect pressure on the political leadership in the form of falling productivity and other passive forms of social resistance; but there were also instances of active and considered resistance against the prevailing social conditions.

Traditionally resistance against the regime has been discussed almost exclusively in connection with the intelligentsia. This of course is due to the fact that the actions of intellectuals and writers, especially with the development of the dissident movement in the 1960s, were the most visible and well formulated, but resistance was much more widespread. This has become more evident with the opening of the archives, where, directly or indirectly, the 'man in the street' is also given voice. Finally it should be stressed that the critical writers and intellectuals in the period in question were not for the most part so critical as to have gone beyond the framework of socialism. Thus in the 1950s there arose something unique in the context of Russia: an alliance between the leaders of government and the critical intelligentsia.

In the following nine chapters a series of stories from Soviet-Russian society in the period 1953–64 are narrated. Each of them in different ways throws light on the kinds of social forces which lay beneath the apparently harmonious surface, and which broke out here and there when Khrushchev loosened the grip of the Party state. With a few exceptions it is average ordinary people, not the critical writers, artists and other members of the intelligentsia about whom so much has been written elsewhere, who are the heroes and anti-heroes of these stories. Some of them were or had been members of the Party, but only a few belonged to the élite.

1
The Closed Letter

Tightening the reins of power

Stalin's death in 1953 and the process of de-Stalinization which followed breathed new life not only into the societies of Eastern Europe but also into Soviet society itself. The uprising in East Berlin, which had already occurred in 1953, and the rebellions in Poland and Hungary which took place respectively in June and October 1956, marked the high points in this revival. All these uprisings were brought to a halt, in the case of the latter by the actual invasion of Soviet troops.

Evidently the events had assumed a direction and a pace which had taken the Kremlin by surprise; those in power saw in them a betrayal of socialism and therefore of their own authority. There is strong evidence to suggest that it was first and foremost the events in Eastern Europe, and particularly in Hungary, which occasioned the Soviet leadership's decision in December 1956 to tighten the reins of power in the Soviet Union, but there were also weighty internal reasons for this shift in policy. The population's dissatisfaction with status quo and demands for change were neither so open nor perhaps so extensive as, for example, in Hungary, but trouble was brewing.

The development of Soviet society after the groundbreaking 20th Party Congress gave rise to concern among a large section of the Party leadership. The critique of Stalin and Stalinism often turned into a critique of the system itself. There were calls at Party meetings for those who had taken part in Stalin's crimes to be severely punished. Demands for freedom and for a firm break with the past were made increasingly boldly by all sections of Soviet society. Reports from local branches of the Party convinced the top leadership that even a modest degree of liberalization had shaken the very foundations of the system, and immediate efforts were made to tighten up. In April 1956, less than a month after the Congress, a special letter was sent out to Party members cautioning them not to overdo their criticism of Stalin. It was followed up by an article in *Pravda* warning against demagogues and other pernicious elements who, under cover of criticizing Stalin, were in fact attacking the Party line itself. Evidently, however, this letter failed to produce the desired effect, for soon afterwards, in July 1956, Party members received a new letter from the Central Committee, this time warning of more severe penalties if the limits of anti-Stalinist criticism were overstepped. Individual offenders were mentioned, and it was reported that a branch of the Party at the Academy of Sciences had been closed down because of their incorrect discussion of the results of the 20th Party Congress.[1] However, there was continued unrest in society at large, and when the disturbances erupted in Hungary in autumn 1956 the Central Committee felt obliged once more to send a warning to Party members. This took the form of a closed letter to Party organizations. This letter, which will be analysed in the following section, was followed by a series of arrests and harsh sentences, under which both Party members and non-Party people were imprisoned for alleged 'revisionism' and anti-Soviet slander. In the first few months of 1957 there were several hundred such arrests, and in an incident in Tbilisi peaceful demonstrators were shot.[2]

The majority of members of the highest Party organ were convinced that these troubles stemmed from the 20th Party Congress. In their view, the problem could only be solved if the Party leadership beat a retreat and thereby undid the damage. There was mounting opposition against Khrushchev, who had obviously taken the lead in the revelations at the Congress. What saved him was that a majority of the members of the Central Committee did not want to see a return to Stalinist methods, and saw in him a guarantee that this would not happen.[3]

By the summer of 1957 opposition to the liberalization within the Presidium had grown to such an extent that a showdown was inevitable. The right wing, led by Molotov, Kaganovich and Malenkov, demanded Khrushchev's resignation. If this wing of the Party had had its way there would certainly have been a return to Stalinist methods, writes the Russian historian V.P. Naumov. In the event this did not happen because the majority of the Central Committee understood that Khrushchev was more in tune with the prevailing mood in society than were his opponents. Naumov writes:

> It was essential to take the mood of the Party and society into consideration. De-Stalinizations and certain steps in the direction of

democratisation were essential, and the condemnation of Stalin's repressions and the arbitrariness of the penal organs was an unavoidable necessity, an expression of the objective social development that took place in the 1950s.[4]

At a meeting of the Presidium in June 1957 the majority of members voted in favour of getting rid of Khrushchev (the Chairman of the Council of Ministers, Bulganin; the Chairman of the Presidium of the Supreme Soviet, Voroshilov, the Deputy Chairmen of the Council of Ministers, Molotov, Kaganovich, Pervukhin and Saburov, and the First Deputy, Malenkov.) Kirichenko, Mikoyan, Suslov and Khrushchev himself voted against his removal. With this threat hanging over him, Khrushchev, with the help of I.A. Serov, mobilized the members of the Central Committee, who streamed into Moscow from all corners of the land. They demanded that the question be taken up at a meeting of the Central Committee itself, and this was duly done. Here it became clear that Khrushchev had the majority behind him, and he thus emerged victorious from a confrontation which was meant to have led to his downfall. Just like Stalin in the 1920s, Khrushchev had understood that he needed to use the local Party leadership in his battle for power. Now it was no longer only the top Party leadership that made up the élite of the country, but the local Party leaders who had seats in the Central Committee. At the meeting, Khrushchev's main opponents, Molotov, Kaganovich and Malenkov were accused of complicity in Stalin's crimes. Despite demands from individual members of the Central Committee to make this accusation known to the public, it was decided that it should be classified as secret. This reaction demonstrated that there were limits to openness. Perhaps the crucial point for Khrushchev was that any such revelation might lead to his coming under the investigators' spotlight himself.

Naumov's interpretation of the political manoeuvrings within the Soviet leadership in the wake of the 20th Party Congress draws, as we have seen, on modernization theory and on Marxist historical analysis in terms of objective social conditions. To be sure, he accords some role in the political game to society, but his account remains at the level of large-scale politics rather than detailed social history. The following section redresses this tendency by looking more closely at the initiatives taken by the political leadership to limit independent activities within society. The leadership was nervous lest such activities ran out of control and undermined the regime. Society's reactions to these initiatives demonstrated that new forces had been released which would not easily be suppressed again.

The letter

At a meeting of the Presidium of the Central Committee of the Communist Party on 19 December 1956 it was decided to send a letter to Party organizations with a note that the contents should be presented and discussed at closed meetings. The title of the letter was clearly indicative of its drift: 'On the strengthening of the Party Organizations' political work among the masses and the halting of activities by anti-Soviet and hostile elements.'[5] Although Party departments were encouraged in the letter to discuss its contents, the overriding impression is that the letter represented a set of unchallengeable instructions rather than a proposal for discussion. In the months after the letter was sent out, the central Party authorities closely monitored the reactions of Party members.

The letter began with a general explanation as to why it was essential that the Party's ideological course and its control over society be tightened. It argued from the premise that developments since the Second World War, with the creation of the so-called People's Democracies in Eastern Europe, had strengthened the contradictions between capitalism and socialism, which had made the capitalist powers nervous and led them to increase their pressure on the socialist countries. Evidence of this could be seen in the uprising in Hungary, which was explained exclusively as a result of ideological propaganda and interference, by the USA and other hostile powers, in Hungary's internal affairs. The uprising had been carried out by a combination of bourgeois capitalist and anti-Soviet elements who were acting against the interests of the Hungarian people.

Much attention was devoted in the letter to 'imperialist propaganda broadcasters' (the BBC and Radio Liberty), which were accused of being in themselves a cause of the outbreak of 'anti-Soviet consciousness' and 'anti-Soviet actions'. As we shall see, there were perhaps genuine grounds for the Soviet authorities' concern over the effect of these radio stations.

Repeated assurances were made that those with 'hostile viewpoints' represented only a very small proportion of the Soviet people, 'the great mass of whom were devoted to socialism'. This statement however is indirectly contradicted by the letter itself and by the whole process which it set in motion, and to a certain extent, directly by the letter's analysis of the internal political situation. It was claimed that several local party leaders had mistakenly received the impression that they no longer had to intervene to prevent 'anti-Soviet activities', and that, for fear of being accused of 'suppressing criticism', they had to far too great an extent allowed it to be expressed. In addition, it was said that many Party members, 'under cover' of their Party membership and of reaction against the cult of personality and its consequences, had begun to criticize the Party line and to demand democracy.

Artists, composers and especially writers were condemned for their more-or-less open demand for artistic freedom. The prominent writer Konstantin Paustovskii (1892-1968) was attacked for having slandered the Soviet government and individual members of the Party leadership at a meeting in the Writers' Union House. This allegedly occurred in connection with a debate on Vladimir Dudintsev's controversial novel *Not by Bread Alone*, which had been published in the autumn of 1956 and was one of the first examples of 'Thaw' literature.

The well-known poet Olga Berggolts (1910–75), who was a Party member, was attacked for having said at a meeting that, in particular, the development of art had been blocked by the decrees on the control of literature issued by the Party in the years immediately after the war, when the notorious Andrei Zhdanov (1896–48) had been at the ideological helm. Criticism of the Party leadership expressed in the journal *Voprosy filosofii* was described as 'objectionable'. Konstantin Simonov (1915–79) himself, and other leading figures in the Writers' Union, were accused of being spokesmen for 'rotten liberalism'. Scholarly journals on history, economics, philosophy and law were criticized in strong terms for not being sufficiently effective in combating 'hostile ideology'. The argument for the Party's continued control over and guidance of art and literature was advanced by quoting Lenin:

> Every artist has the right to create freely in accordance with his ideal, totally independently. But it goes without saying that we are communists, we can't just stand there and watch chaos developing. We have to steer the whole process and shape its results in a properly planned way.[6]

The quotation is typical of Lenin's contradictory way of expressing himself, which may have been one reason why it was possible to use his words as justification both for tightening and for loosening the Party's grip on society. This ambiguity also lay at the heart of the dilemma in which Khrushchev found himself. On the one hand he was aware of the need to slacken the reins; on the other he was a communist and could not therefore simply operate a *laissez-faire* policy when developments took an unexpected turn.

The attack on the intelligentsia was especially sharp and appears more in accordance with the tone of the postwar years than with the spirit of the 20th Party Congress. In reality the demands made by writers for tolerable conditions for literature and art were moderate, and the attack in the letter should be seen as an expression of the Party leadership's general nervousness lest control of society should slip out of their hands.

A significant part of the letter was devoted to youth. An increase in spontaneous activities, accompanied by 'anti-Soviet opinions' and 'wrong points of view', was noted particularly among students. At the universities of Moscow, Sverdlovsk and Kaunas, as well as several other places, this had led to anti-Soviet and nationalist demonstrations. In Estonia demands had been voiced at a student meeting for independent national youth organizations, and the 'Hungarian counter-revolution' was applauded. At the university of Erevan, the capital of Armenia, local communists had come out with declarations directed against the Party, and under the guise of condemning the cult of personality these had raised a question mark over the Party and government's policies.

The Central Committee took the view that the problems with youth had arisen because the Party had not done its work well enough. Young people had not been sufficiently deeply imbued with socialist values, including an understanding of the falsity of bourgeois ideology and the threat it posed. This superficial analysis and the rather hopeless solutions proposed were characteristic of the general level of awareness expressed both in the Central Committee's letter, and in the reports of the discussions which followed it in local branches of the Party.

The Central Committee suggested that the local authorities should keep a vigilant eye on the many thousands of people who since Stalin's death, and especially after 1955, had been released from prison camps. Party organizations were ordered to keep watch especially on 'Mensheviks' and 'bourgeois nationalists' who, it was claimed, nurtured an inveterate hatred towards Soviet power, and many of whom had resumed their so-called 'socially damaging' activities since their release.

One question which arises on reading the Central Committee's letter is whether it represents an expression of the political leadership's true understanding of the international situation and internal social problems, or an ideological construction for propaganda purposes. In other words, did the leaders know more, and perhaps understand the situation better, than they revealed in the letter? The question cannot be conclusively answered, but there are several indications that this was the case.

Firstly from the reports sent to the Soviet leadership by the ambassador in Budapest it was evident that the uprising had significant *popular* backing. Against this background the description of the events in the Central Committee's letter appears very distorted and tendentious.[7] Secondly, Khrushchev's son-in-law, Adzubei, writes in his memoirs that his father-in-law quickly recognized that the uprising in Hungary was not just brought about by a small group of counter-revolutionaries in and outside the country, but had broad popular support. According to Adzubei, a decisive factor in Khrushchev's decision to send troops into Hungary, however, was that he was concerned about the internal political situation in the Soviet Union itself, which had arisen as a result of the 20th Party Congress. Adzubei writes: 'The country was seething and boiling. Meetings were held at which extreme demands were put forward, including the idea of arming the population.'[8]

If Adzubei's information is to be believed, it suggests that the ideological outlook, which characterizes the first part of the letter, was merely an attempt to explain away the internal reasons for dissatisfaction with the regime. This dissatisfaction, as we have discussed, had arisen in the wake of the 20th Party Congress, and was evidently significant enough to make it neccesary for the Soviet regime not merely to take action against developments in the neighbouring states of Poland and Hungary, but also to start an internal campaign against its own population. Without doubt the crisis in Hungary had demonstrated that the system itself was at risk if the Party sought to modernize. Thus the Party leadership 'went into reverse' and resorted in this case to tried and tested means.

The letter can thus be seen as a lengthy demonstration of the Central Committee's more-or-less vain attempt to rein in the developments which were thought to have been set in motion by the 20th Party Congress. It is undoubtedly the case that the Party Congress made a significant contribution to reducing fear, but some critical awareness must have been present among the population before the Congress too.

Society's reactions to the letter

Below we shall see how the leaders of the Party's grassroots organizations and individual members received the Central Committee's letter. We should of course be clear at the outset that we are speaking here of a rather special segment of Soviet society – what might be called the Party public. This cannot be directly identified with Soviet society in general, but it is not unreasonable to suppose that Party members in their association with other Soviet citizens were influenced by the spirit of the times and thus also gave expression to those opinions and attitudes which were generally current. When some Party members, as we shall see, expressed 'anti-Soviet' views at meetings, one might claim – as the reports on these meetings repeatedly did – that such people were exceptions, or intoxicated individuals who had forgotten where they were. Their behaviour however could also be interpreted as arising from the fact that the disappearance of fear had led them finally to say out loud what was really in their hearts. It might also be argued that when Party members themselves stepped over the line, it was because pressure from the society around them was increasing: it was particularly outside the Party public that the new language and new consciousness were created.

The Central Committee watched closely to see how ordinary Party members received the letter. They did so with the help of minutely detailed reports from local Party meetings where it had been presented. Some of these reports went straight to the Central Committee, but most landed up in various sub-departments, where they were analysed, summarized and commented on. There is little doubt that the whole of this apparatus, which was set in motion when important questions were on the agenda, functioned primarily as a link in the Party's totalitarian control of society. Nevertheless, one cannot exclude the possibility that through this means popular opinion may have played a certain role in the central authorities' decisions. In either case, what is important is that the reports reflected the population's attitudes and were not just messages fabricated by their senders to tell the central authorities what they wanted to hear, or manufactured by local Party leaders to cover up their lack of control in their own local areas. There are numerous indications, from various periods throughout the history of the Soviet state, to confirm that the Party leadership paid great attention to the problem of getting reliable feedback about society. The Party's efforts to gather information from different sources, such as Party branches, the KGB and other organizations, also testify to this. The information problem was, however, never solved, and this most probably constituted an important factor in the break-up of the system.

V. Churaev, who was the leader of the Central Committee's department for Party organizations, introduced his first report to the Central Committee on 9 January 1957 by assuring them that the closed letter had been eagerly discussed by Party organizations at all levels of society, and that the Communists, who saw it as an important document in strengthening both unity within the Party and the Party's influence on the masses, had unanimously approved it. In support of this statement he presented numerous pronouncements from ordinary Party members who had been disturbed by developments in society since the 20th Party Congress, by the rejection of the 'cult of personality' and by the events in Hungary.[9] All of this had led, it was claimed, to an outbreak of demagogic talk and anti-Soviet jokes. It was however stressed that these anti-Soviet pronouncements and attitudes were mere drops in the great sea of staunch unity within the Party ranks and indeed society as a whole. This pattern was typical of all these reports.

Churaev confirmed the Central Committee's worries over the harmful influence in the Soviet Union of Western radio stations. Particular emphasis was put on the radio station 'Voice of America'. It was added that the growing influx of Western tourists had a similarly negative effect, and that Soviet youth, in particular, was especially at risk from the West's cunning propaganda, and needed to be protected.

It is evident that there was great doubt generally over how the message of the 20th Party Congress should be interpreted. The report claimed that statements of criticism and self-criticism, the repudiation of the cult of personality, and the reintroduction of Lenin's principles of Party life and collective leadership had prevented many from intervening against deviant pronouncements and behaviour. It was alleged that several local leaders and Party members mistakenly believed that the message of the Party Congress amounted to a call for 'free discussion' of Party policy. It was also claimed that prior to the letter Communists had been reluctant to counter criticisms, slander and hostile propaganda for fear of being accused of suppressing criticism. The Central Committee's letter set things in their proper place. Their judgement was backed up with statements expressing relief that the 'time of troubles' was over. At a meeting of a factory committee in Vladivostok a worker named Moskalev was alleged to have said: 'The Central Committee's letter obliged every Communist to strengthen his political convictions and liquidate his petty-bourgeois insouciance.' That this alleged insouciance had been able to take root at all was surely not merely a result of signals from above. It could not have developed so quickly and become a problem for the Party if there had not already been fertile ground for it.

The reports also confirmed the Central Committee's concern over developments among young people. It was especially emphasized on all sides that the Party should pay greater attention to youth and particularly to the Communist organization Komsomol. It was revealed that at the pedagogical institute in Kirov 16 students were exchanging letters with foreign students and had recently received strongly anti-Soviet letters from Poland and France, which were being circulated at the Institute. The local Party organization received a strong reprimand for not having been sufficiently vigilant and stopped these developments in time. As evidence of the critical mood among students, an intervention by a student named Rykov, at a meeting at the historical-philological faculty at Kursk Pedagogical Institute, was reported in full:

'Komsomol is a boring organization, and if I were to decide whether to become a member now, I wouldn't join. It demands only that we work and study, and there's no fun in it. If they don't pay attention to young people, it will lead to the kind of events we saw in Hungary. I demand freedom for youth.'

Many expressed the view that the problem with youth would be solved if access to higher educational institutions were regulated, so that a higher proportion of students from worker or peasant backgrounds were brought in. The majority of students were the children of civil servants, who, it was claimed, knew nothing of either work or life. This kind of solution had its origins in the socialist dogma that young working-class people, by virtue of their class affiliation, were more in tune with Party policy. Yet this relationship was not perhaps as self-evident and mechanical as it might appear at first sight. On the basis of his investigations, an American researcher has concluded that those among young people whose career was dependent on membership of Komsomol and the Party, and on 'correct behaviour' in the public arena, were more conformist than others. In other words there was a tendency for young people in higher education in the major cities to be – at any rate outwardly – more ready to go along with the Party line than young people elsewhere.[10]

At a meeting on 21 December 1956 the leader of the Moscow city legal office, Kozyrev, who was a member of the Party, made a critical intervention, which was later, included in Churaev's report:

'Today we discuss problems with political agitation, but we don't see the most important thing. We only talk about the resolutions from the 20th Party Congress, but nobody does anything … . We only have democracy on paper: the elections to all the governing organs are only democratic in form, in reality we only have the right to vote. We are still afraid to criticize, because there is still a risk that we may end up in prison [for doing so]. We should pay more heed to the experience of countries such as Yugoslavia and Hungary and learn from them how to build socialism.'[11]

Kozyrev delivered a consciously formulated criticism of the system and of the lack of coherence in the reforms, and concluded with a demand for democratic rights. There were thus good grounds for reporting on him and, in the case of the local branch of the Party, discussing his expulsion from the Party. It is much more difficult to understand why Churaev found it necessary to report on the further development of the case. The outcome was rather astonishing. Following his intervention, Kozyrev was called in to a meeting of the Party bureau, where he expressed regret at his words and excused them on the grounds that he had been very drunk. After some discussion it was decided that he could remain in the Party.

The numerous statements gathered from meetings around the country were designed to provide evidence that the general line of the Party, as expressed in the letter, had the backing of the rank and file. Other quotations, on the other hand, would demonstrate the need for further efforts on the ideological front, and the appropriateness therefore of the Central Committee's action. Churaev gave assurances that the Party had the situation under control, and there is no reason to doubt this, just as there is no reason to doubt that the 'anti-Soviet elements' – people who openly expressed views that differed from the Party line – were the clear minority. However, what people said and did was one thing; what they thought was quite another. Several statements in the reports indicate that people were still afraid to express their opinions, and this suggests that 'anti-Soviet elements' may have been more numerous than appeared at first sight. It is reasonable to suppose that only the bravest, or the most naive, dared to come out with their criticisms.

The proposals from Party organizations that problems should be solved simply by increased propaganda efforts and stricter control were quite routine, and few can have seriously believed that these solutions would help. The discussions appear both monotonous and ritualistic, as do the resolutions which resulted from them. The main points of the letter are simply reiterated, occasionally with minor additions. Altogether one gets the impression of a tired apparatus, lacking either spirit or faith in its own undertakings.

Churaev's second report begins with a routine assurance that the Central Committee's letter had received widespread approval at meetings of the Party's local branches.[12] It was again stressed that there were only a few Communists who had not behaved correctly at the meetings and made interventions that were critical of the Party and government. Nevertheless, the greater part of the report was devoted precisely to these critical statements.

At a meeting of the Party organization at the hydro-electric power station in Kuibyshev, a candidate member of the Party, Dubrovin, had criticized the Party's interference in literature and art and remarked not only that this was unnecessary but that it was also embarrassing and hateful. On the same occasion, moreover, he criticized the Party leadership for visiting only the most prosperous *kolkhozes*. Thus Molotov, for example, had recently been to dinner with a well-off local family. At the same meeting a brigade leader, Politov, related that certain workers who listened to the Western radio station 'Svobodnaya Evropa' had found out that the leader of the building works at the hydro-electric station, Komzin, had received a 50,000 rouble bonus and a fine car. He concluded his intervention by saying that those who lived best and earned most were not those who worked, but those who signed papers. At a meeting of the Party organization in the town of Kuibyshev a pensioner named Taganov had made a speech criticizing living standards. He said: 'On those posters where they talk about unemployment and poverty in the capitalist countries the heading should be changed!'

The above interventions were not opposed at the meeting itself. A member of the Party organization's bureau, however, dismissed one critical remark out of hand. Nevertheless, later the City Committee (*gorkom*) in Stavropol took action and expelled the critical members, and the Party bureau was disbanded. This occurred not only because they had been unable to make sure that Party discipline was maintained among the rank-and-file members, but also-and especially-because it was known that several of the leading members often took part in drinking bouts.

Churaev's third report begins, like the two previous ones, with a statement that stability prevailed, but, as we shall see, the critical statements it contained were more far-reaching and hard-hitting than those seen hitherto. At a Party meeting at the car factory in Yaroslavl the chief engineer, Kiselev, made an intervention that was characterized as anti-Soviet. Deeply frustrated by the Central Committee's letter, he said that now, once again, the slogan was: 'Either you shut up, or you'll be locked up.' He wondered, moreover, why the Soviet press, unlike the Chinese, had not published Tito's speeches, and he asked the other participants in the meeting if this was because Soviet citizens were more stupid than the Chinese. He also took the view that the Party in Hungary were themselves to blame for what had gone wrong, although in his opinion the Hungarian communists had committed only a fraction of the mistakes committed by the leadership of the Soviet Communist Party. He then went into the social situation in the Soviet Union and expressed the view that the difference between rich and poor had become much greater than it had been before the revolution. In those days the ratio between the poorest and the richest had been 1:20; Lenin had brought it down to 1:5, but in 1957, according to Kiselev, it was 1:100. He concluded his intervention by quoting a French worker who had visited his factory: 'It is better to die than to live as you live here.'

The report reveals that in all 11 members spoke at the meeting. Some backed Kiselev up and praised him for his courage and honesty, others criticized his speech and dubbed it anti-Soviet. Finally a vote was taken on whether Kiselev's intervention should indeed be characterized anti-Soviet. Seventeen voted in favour, 21 against, and 18 declined to vote.

Churaev was very critical of the local Party leadership's procedures in relation to Kiselev. Instead of allowing a vote on his intervention, which, as we have seen, gave him support, the leadership should have immediately condemned it as anti-Soviet. Kiselev was later called to a meeting in the *gorkom* (City Committee) where he was asked to explain himself. He repeated his criticism of the Party leadership and of conditions in the country, and gave it an even sharper twist. Among other things he said that the Party had reached a critical age, and that far too many scoundrels and careerists had got to the top. Not surprisingly, the *gorkom* decided after this to expel him from the Party.

The report contains a further example of anti-Soviet activity from Yaroslavl. At a meeting in a factory committee, one of the workers criticized the Party leadership for not thinking about the workers' conditions, and Bulganin was accused of doing nothing but holding banquets. The worker concluded by saying that conditions in the USA were much better than in the Soviet Union.

The report also revealed that the Central Committee had sent an inspector named Simonov to Yaroslavl to assist the Gorkom in improving its propaganda efforts among the local branches of the Party. This may be seen as an indication that the opposition was more widespread than was claimed in the reports.

From Saratov it was reported that the Raikom (District Committee) had expelled from the Party the chief engineer at a shipyard for having remarked, at a meeting of the shipyard's branch of the Party, that the standard of living in the Soviet Union was lower than in Africa, as well as making various critical remarks about the KGB.

A report from Bryansk meanwhile concerns some unfortunate statements made by a number of students at the forestry institute. A student named Mayorov, born in 1935, said at a seminar that the claims that the Soviet Union would overtake the capitalist countries economically were empty. Soviet power had not improved the lot of the oppressed Russian peasants, and whereas workers in the USA could buy a car, not even an engineer in the Soviet Union could dream of doing so. A student named Efanov said at the same meeting that the standard of living in the Soviet Union was below subsistence level. The leader of the seminar attempted to counter these critical statements by presenting positive examples from Soviet life and commending Soviet literature. The students, however, were not sympathetic: 'We know what they write in books. We have gorged ourselves on books!'

The critical students were not contradicted at the seminar itself, and the Party bureau at the Institute therefore called a meeting. However, this initiative came to nothing, since no one apart from the bureau's leaders attended. At a subsequent meeting Majorov spoke up and defended himself as follows:

> 'It is possible that in certain cases I think like Trotskii, but you must convince me and not simply reject me … . For example, I don't understand why in 1913 one could eat white bread, while today one must stand in line to buy black bread, and why a peasant from the *kolkhoz* has to come to the city to get the grain which he has delivered to the state.'

Mayorov's intervention testifies clearly to the inadequacy of the Party's propaganda and its methods of education. Its arguments were too weak and abstract to convince the students, and since its methods of control went no further than throwing critical students out of Komsomol, the Party in practice was unable to deter this kind of behaviour.

We now turn to a particular report from the Party secretary in Moscow, N. Kapitonov (1957).[13] It provides a very clear indication of the extensive measures that were taken. First, instruction meetings were held for all leaders at *raikom* (District committee) and *gorkom* level. These leaders then brought the information back to their organizations, which in turn sent instructions out to the organizations at the grassroots. In Stalinogorsk, 53 branches of the Party, in which at least 90 per cent of Party members took part, held meetings.

What follows shows clearly how the religious community still posed a threat to Soviet power. At a factory meeting a Party functionary named

Nefedov related observing Baptist gatherings at the home of an elderly worker named Voloshina who lived in Room 30, Barrack 14, where anti-Soviet discussions had taken place and slanderous rumours circulated. He explained how the Baptists, by playing on the housing situation, had gained a certain influence among the rest of the workers in the barracks. At the meeting it was decided, by way of a counter-measure, to send various politically conscious agitators out to the workers' barracks to put a stop to the Baptists' activities and influence. This decision testifies once again to the Communists' feeble methods of preventing opposition from spreading. An improvement in housing conditions would doubtless have been a great deal more effective than even the best anti-religious propaganda.

At the same meeting a joiner named Kabanov made a speech criticizing the factory management. He argued that the campaign for better discipline should start from above, and complained in this connection that the director of the factory and several leading employees frequently came to work in a state of intoxication, which in his view had a very negative effect on the morale of the whole working collective. A worker named Rybakov likewise attacked the factory elite. He accused the bosses and foremen of using only swear words and obscenities in dealing with the younger workers, and of tempting the younger ones into drinking. A propaganda worker named Borisov reported from a mine employing 400 young miners, of whom 200 were members of Komsomol, that the level of culture, even among young Communists, was very low, and drinking was widespread. Borisov proposed that the sale of vodka should be reduced and that the local shop should no longer fulfil its plan for trade through increasing vodka sales, but by increasing the sale of foodstuffs. In the light of what we know about the appalling overall situation with regard to supplies, this was more easily said than done.

These criticisms were not deemed anti-Soviet. If they were included in Kapitonov's report it was perhaps because in his view this was the kind of criticism which the new openness should be used for.

V. Tishchenko, who was employed in the central Party apparatus, focused in his report on the fact that rumours of everything ranging from imminent price rises to a new world war were far too easily spread, and that Party members were too reluctant to put a stop to them; indeed, on occasion they themselves helped to spread them.[14] From the reports he had gathered from local Party organizations, it emerged that the main sources of these rumours were broadcasts in Russian from 'Voice of America' and the BBC.

According to local Party leaders, the Soviet press was not properly equipped to counter the propaganda from these foreign radio stations. Agitators moreover were often too poorly educated to be able to do anything effective about it. Most of the leaders urged that jamming stations be set up, but some were more democratically inclined and took the view that the Soviet media should attempt to enter the competition by improving their own output.

Many Party members believed that since the 20th Congress the mass media had been far too busy revealing administrative irregularities, or criticizing bureaucracy in the state and Party institutions, and had therefore neglected to promote the positive sides of Soviet life. Tishchenko drew on demands from local branches of the Party to urge that the educative and propaganda function of the press be strengthened. He was conscious of the fact that this might appear to be at variance with the declarations of the 20th Party Congress concerning criticism and self-criticism, but he defended it on the grounds that the press had gone further than had been intended.

Tishchenko devoted much attention to describing the 'critical attitude' among young people at institutes of higher education. Thus it emerged that at public meetings at the Molotov State University, young Communists had openly made speeches undermining Soviet power and the CPSU. An intervention by a student at a Komsomol meeting is cited in this connection: 'All of you are cowards and hypocrites. You whisper in corners that communism is just a new religion; but you keep your mouths shut here.'

At a seminar about the history of the CPSU, a member of the Komsomol named Schnaider asked if it was possible that the events in Hungary would set off a counter-revolution in the Soviet Union. When the teacher denied this, one of the students was heard to say: 'What a pity!'

At a history seminar two students named Eisfeld and Baranov aired their view that the 'personality cult' was a consequence of the one-party system, and compared developments in Germany and the Soviet Union under Hitler and Stalin respectively. In their opinion, the only safeguards against the cult of personality were parliamentary democracy and freedom of expression. Describing the two critics, the report claimed: 'Eisfeld and Baranov contrast our Soviet system with so-called Western democracy. They maintain that a political leader can win genuine authority among the masses only in a multiparty system.' Tishchenko observed that neither the teachers nor the professors had taken such opposition sufficiently seriously, and that it had been reported far too late. In his view, the reason for this was that many of the teachers had misunderstood the critique of the cult of personality, and had therefore allowed students to do and say whatever they wanted. Other teachers and professors were accused of concerning themselves only with criticizing the system rather than pointing out what the Party was doing to improve it.

Tishchenko realized that some people would fear that the letter would put a stop to any form of criticism, although he himself was convinced that this was not the intention. He was uncompromising, however, in his view of those who, he considered, had misused the letter for anti-Soviet agitation. One such person, in his opinion, was the director of Gorkii House, Tereshnikov, who had said at a meeting:

> 'If a machine were invented that could X-ray people's brains, it would show that 70–80 per cent of people don't approve of the existing order in our country. On one side is luxury, on the other poverty! The 20th Party Congress loosened many people's tongues. People began bravely expressing their dissatisfaction. But this letter is a return to the time before the congress.'

V. Kannunikov, who was the leader of the Pskov *obkom* (Regional Committee), introduced his report with a statistical summary concerning the number of meetings held in connection with the letter from the Central Committee. This revealed that as of 14 January 1957, 777 closed meetings had been held by grassroots Party organizations, which amounted to 55 per cent of the total. He explained that 7,592 out of 8,737 members had taken part in the meetings, and of these 2,776 had spoken.[15] In her account, a woman named Polonskaya from the Party organization in Pskov said that people who had consciously aimed to undermine the authority of the Party and state had recently begun to behave too freely, and that the Party needed to take the most decisive measures against such people.

At a series of meetings held by Party committees in the surrounding villages, members brought up the problem of rumour-mongering. In recent years, for example, there had been several reports that a currency reform was imminent, which had led to local shops quickly being emptied of all purchaseable goods. In the wake of the Hungarian crisis persistent rumours had arisen of a coming war. At a *kolkhoz* there had been a discussion about what measures should be taken against a *kolkhoz* member named Sobolev, who was known to have a radio receiver and to have organized collective sessions listening to broadcasts from 'Voice of America'. The same Sobolev had on several occasions threatened the *kolkhoz* chairman that he would be hanged from the nearest birch tree as soon as 'our rule is established'.

The Pskov region had the particular problem that local people often visited the Soviet republic of Estonia and returned with all sorts of malicious rumours about Soviet power. The report claimed that these rumours were often believed, because the Party and Komsomol were not sufficiently energetic in their educational work. Several *kolkhozes* reported that they virtually never saw representatives from the highest Party organs in the city, and that this was the reason for the relatively low level of political consciousness in the villages. Some of the reports stated directly that the local propaganda workers were not very bright.

Finally we will look at a report from Bryansk, where 1,003 grassroots organizations (43 per cent) had held meetings about the Central Committee's letter. Only 3 per cent of members, however, had spoken at these meetings.[16] In Bryansk, as in Pskov, there was heavy criticism of the lack of communication between the central and the local Party organizations. As an example it was mentioned that, in connection with the Suez crisis in Egypt and the crisis in Hungary, numerous questions had arisen among workers and *kolkhoz* peasants which local Party secretaries had been unable to answer. This was also the case after the 20th Party Congress, when workers at various factories round the city had voiced strong attacks against Stalin, which local Party people had been unable to do anything about. The problem, it was claimed, was that 'they did not even know themselves how to interpret the concept of "the cult of personality".'

It was indicated that there were problems in explaining the Party's and government's policies to the population. The authors themselves laid the blame on a lack of competence among local Party people, but the reason may also have been that ordinary people had begun to ask questions and put forward criticisms that could not be answered or countered even by a trained agitator from the city.

An increase in anti-Soviet activity, especially among former political prisoners, had been noticed in different districts and regions. At the cement factory in Bryansk it had been observed that railway wagons often arrived bearing 'hostile graffiti'. At the '1st May' *kolkhoz* handwritten leaflets had been distributed urging *kolkhoz* members not to subjugate themselves to the *kolkhoz* chairman, and not to go to work. The leaflet also contained a threat to murder the *kolkhoz* chairman if he did not leave the *kolkhoz*.

The Central Committee's secret letter may be seen as an expression of concern on the part of the leadership that the crisis in Hungary would spread to the Soviet Union. The statements in the reports, to the effect that the overwhelming majority of Party members were loyal, may have been reassuring, but could not do away with the fact that there was a critical number among the Party and the population who did not hesitate to express even strongly critical attitudes towards the system, and who declared themselves dissatisfied with the change of course that had been set in motion at the 20th Party Congress.

It is highly unlikely that the increasing 'anti-Soviet activity' was solely a result of indulgence, lack of effective propaganda, and the harmful influence of the foreign media and tourists, as the Central Committee claimed. Rather, it was an indication that fear had diminished, and that the potential criticisms, which had long been present but could not previously be formulated, had now been unleashed.

We have seen that certain Party leaders hankered after stronger propaganda and more control. This in itself, like the letter from the Central Committee, was a sign of growing unrest within society. It is questionable whether information and propaganda, no matter how brilliant, would have been sufficient to quell this unrest. Could propaganda, in other words, have explained the many unfairnesses and absurdities to which the population had been subjected? It could not, and Khrushchev's grandiose attempt to effect a shift from an outward to an internal form of control was therefore doomed to failure. The political leaders attempted to explain and rectify things, but they were overwhelmed by the irrationality of the system, and in order to retain their power were forced to resort to the well-tried methods of increased surveillance and control.

It is unlikely that those who wrote the reports to the Central Committee were deliberately concealing the truth when they assured the leadership that the great majority of the population applauded the Party's policies. However, if they were really convinced of this, it seems strange that they devoted so much attention to the modest number of people who did not toe the Party line or were directly opposed to it. Could this perhaps have been an indication of the view they themselves took? In that case, the reports could be seen as a means of communicating the message further: this is how things are in reality, but we do not dare to say so ourselves!

2
The Church and the State

During the Khrushchev period, Party policy in relation to the Russian Orthodox Church alternated between greater strictness and liberalization. The more repressive policies which eventually won the day were the result of the Party's general plans for modernization, in which no room had been left for religion or for other so-called 'primitive forms of consciousness'. The tough line towards the Church and religious believers met with considerable popular resistance and undoubtedly contributed to the discrediting of Khrushchev's regime in the eyes of the population. It ran so contrary to the overall policy of the Thaw that it led people to doubt the real intentions of the political leadership.

By the end of the 1930s, despite two decades of grim psychological and physical struggle against the Orthodox Church and religious believers, which had led to the destruction of the vast majority of Russian churches, monasteries and seminaries, the Soviet authorities, led by Stalin, were forced to admit that their efforts had been in vain. Thus the 1937 census revealed that more than 50 per cent of the population acknowledged themselves to be believers.[1] Considering the persecution to which believers were subject, it was surprising that such a large number should by this means have more or less openly declared themselves, and the real figure may well have been higher. The results of this census doubtless contributed strongly to Stalin's decision to introduce a policy of co-operation with the Church and with believers, a policy which became especially evident after Germany's attack on the Soviet Union in the summer of 1941. The political leaders appear to have recognized that religion and other traditional values were a better tool for mobilizing the population than was socialist ideology. In 1943 the authorities went so far as to reopen several monasteries and seminaries.

35

During the war many congregations spontaneously opened their churches without the state taking action to prevent their doing so.

When Stalin died in 1953, Church leaders and believers were worried that pre-war policies would be reintroduced. It was obvious that Stalin, after initially wavering, had been more pragmatic over this question than most of the other leading communists. These fears proved justified. By 1954, on Khrushchev's own initiative, a decree had been issued which marked the end of the policy of co-operation with the Church. The population reacted so strongly to the decree, however, that the authorities were forced soon afterwards to abandon this hard line. Another reason for this turnabout was presumably that the political leadership had recognized that the Church could be used in the Soviet Union's 'Peace policy'.

The changes were expressed in a decree issued by the Central Committee on 10 November 1954. There is no doubt that the Party's goal was still to stamp out religious faith, but this should be brought about, as they put it, by other and more modern methods. In connection with the publication of the decree a number of measures were taken by central and local Party organ to disseminate information and educate 'agitators' who subsequently, at Party meetings in local branches, workplaces and clubs, would explain the meaning of the decree to the population and discuss any questions that arose. Reports from these meetings were used to measure how the population had received the Central Committee's initiatives. Thus in Kaliningrad region 150 Party agitators were sent out to factories and institutions, where the decree was read aloud and discussions between the agitators and those attending took place. It was reported that 15,000 people took part in these meetings.[2]

Popular reactions

The reports to the Central Committee concerning the population's reactions followed the familiar pattern. First, assurances were made that a broad section of society supported the Party's policies. Representatives of the people then presented evidence for this claim through a series of positive statements. At the same time the reports departed from the usual practice in dealing with decrees by discarding the manner in which the Party had treated the question hitherto. It was directly acknowledged that the Party had behaved wrongly in its fight against religion, and this acknowledgement met with a sympathetic response in the statements made at the meetings. A woman from a *kolkhoz* in the Leningrad region declared: 'The Central Committee's decree is good, but it would have been better if it had come earlier. In our *kolkhoz*, instead of being told why we shouldn't believe in God, we were ordered not to believe in God and not to go to church.'[3]

This and other statements indicate a critical attitude towards the Party's policy which could be expressed only after the decree was issued. The same went for the many complaints about the poor level of education among the anti-religious agitators and the primitive level of their propaganda, which had simply irritated believers. A weaver from Ivanovo relates how an agitator who was meant to come to a residents' association meeting and tell participants about the origins of religion, had instead used the time to talk about how badly priests behaved and how much they earned.

True to form, the reports also gave space to examples of opposition to the Party line, but as always these are characterized as sporadic and one-off, and as absolute exceptions to the rule. Opinions and attitudes which, prior to the Party's decree, had been regarded as exemplary were now all at once seen as an expression of deviance. A worker from Omsk is rebuked for the following statement: 'I live next to the church on Rabinovich Street and see how the priest drinks and staggers about. All churches should be closed immediately.'

Some of the reports expressed fears that a milder policy on religion would mean that many would begin to go to church again. Some districts reported that Party members had understood the decree to mean that they could now begin to go to church with a clear conscience and have their children christened. Both these assumptions were rejected as misunderstandings of the Party line.

More serious heed was paid to those opponents who claimed that the Central Committee's decree was not sincerely meant, and that it represented merely a tactical move to strengthen the regime's legitimacy both internally and in relation to the West. Mintsuk, a member of a sect in the Irkutsk region, is reported to have said: 'Churchill said that if the Soviet government had not fought religion, there would be no more powerful state on earth than the Soviet Union. Soviet politicians will soon understand this and then there will be religious freedom.' A Moslem named Araslanov from Molotov was much more sceptical: 'The whole thing is a fraud. They're pretending to do something for ordinary people in order to damp down criticism from the West.' As we shall see, these remarks were not unfounded.

Some leading Bolsheviks recognized early on that the Party could not fight religion merely by closing churches.[4] It was believed that the ritual of the Church had an important social therapeutic function, especially in the dreary, prospectless everyday life of the poor, and that something which could compete with the spectacle provided by the Church therefore had to be found: something which had an equivalent power to attract, but which avoided the damaging ideological content of religion. Heavy investment in film and cinema should be recognized as one answer to this problem; but workers' clubs and the whole organization of the rest of life outside the work-place were also relevant here. The reports show that little progress had been made in creating social alternatives to the Church. Whereas the churches were well-maintained and clean, and many of them were heated in winter, the workers' clubs were badly kept. They were messy, dirty and cold. Complaints were also made that there were never any events on offer for adults, and that the clubs were used only by young people for holding parties. The state registry offices were also criticized for being dull and lacking in ceremony, and this was put forward as the direct cause of the fact that young people were beginning to get married in church.

In the commentaries to the reports, optimistic assurances are made that the local branches of the Party would correct these failures. This would happen, for example, through better training of club workers. This kind of superficial solution to what were, in fact, serious problems for the Party was typical, and can scarcely have been seriously intended. On the other hand, it represented more or less the only suggestion the report writers could come up with when the system blocked any more profound analysis of the problems involved.

The resolution did not mean, as some naively believed, that the Party would cease its fight against religion and the Church, but only that its methods should be modernized. As suggested above, it is evident from the reports that the ignorance of the propagandists and the primitive level of anti-religious propaganda meant that the latter had not hitherto been taken seriously, and indeed – for the same reasons – had been counter-productive and strengthened people in their religious beliefs. Two of the reports moreover drew attention to the fact that atheist propaganda was almost exclusively carried out at Party meetings and workers' clubs, where religious believers were never to be seen.

Open confrontation

In the late 1950s a renewed offensive against the Orthodox Church and religious believers was launched. The reason, allegedly, was that there had been a sharp increase in the number of believers openly taking part in church ceremonies and other religious activities. The reactions to this offensive show that believers were not inclined to submit to Party policy voluntarily, and when the results were assessed after the fall of Khrushchev in 1964, it had to be acknowledged that Party policy in this area had in fact been counter-productive.

The authorities' forcible closure of churches and monasteries met with broad popular resistance, and now and then led to violent confrontations. Monks and priests had to be forcibly led away by a powerful array of volunteer police (*druzhinniki*), militia and soldiers. Church services were disrupted and parishioners chased away by means of threats and sometimes even physical force. In June 1961 the Glinskii monastery was closed, an action in which 250 militia, volunteer police, KGB agents and Party activists took part. Later that year the authorities in the Chernopol Region were informed that the number of monks at the Potayevskaya monastery had been reduced from 130 to 75, but that the monks had barricaded themselves into the monastery and refused to leave. As news of the authorities' activities spread through the country, the number of visitors and pilgrims coming to the monastery in connection with religious festivals rose significantly. In 1963 a crowd of 5,000 pilgrims was forcibly dispersed. When news of this incident reached the West, the KGB intervened and advised the Central Committee to give up the enterprise. Thereafter the monastery was left in peace.

When a new Party programme was approved at the 22nd Party Congress in 1961, heralding the advent of communism in the Soviet Union within 20 years, Khrushchev declared that he would soon be presenting a museum piece on television: the last priest in Russia.

Between 1960 and 1962 the number of clashes between the authorities and believers increased drastically. As many as 30 per cent of churches were destroyed, and the number of monasteries fell by 25 per cent. From 1961 to 1962, complaints to the Party authorities concerning the use of violence in closing down churches rose from 1,549 to 2,660.[5] In 1962 several thousand believers resisted the removal of the cross from a church which had been closed by the authorities a short time previously. Two hundred members of the auxiliary police and around 100 armed soldiers took part in the action against them.

Between 1962 and 1963 there was a lull in the authorities' anti-religious activities. This has been explained by growing economic problems and the Cuba missile crisis, which meant that the authorities needed to cultivate a better image externally. In 1964, however, the hard line was resumed fully. In this connection Stalin's 'policy of reconciliation' (1943–53) was condemned as a deviation from Leninism. Believers were quick to react. The Council for Religious Affairs, a state organization, reported to the Central Committee that the Church authorities were preparing to resist, and that there were rumours that they were ready to submit to the authority of the Pope in Rome in order to get the support of the Roman Catholic Church. 'Better submit to the Pope', it was said, 'than to this godless power'. The KGB meanwhile reported that the number of illegal religious documents had risen sharply, and in Leningrad the first example of an illegal political-religious organization could be seen in the form of 'The All-Russian Social Christian Union for the Liberation of the People' (Vserossiiskii Sotsial-Khristyanskii Soyuz Osvobozhdeniya Naroda).

The pressure on the Party came not only from within the borders of the Soviet Union but also from outside. Awareness had spread abroad that there was a darker side to Khrushchev's Thaw policy. In 1964 both the French and the Italian communists made protests.

The Church authorities and religious believers identified Party and government policy with Khrushchev, and this unpopular offensive thus led to a sharp decline in his personal authority. When Khrushchev was removed from power in 1964, hopes arose for a milder policy towards the Church. The Council for Religious Affairs in Leningrad reported that surveillance of churches ceased spontaneously. During the first half of 1964, when Khrushchev was still in power, 575 people had been baptized in the Trinity Church. On 18 October 53 were baptized in a single day.[6]

According to the Russian researcher Shkarovskii, the new Party leaders feared nothing less than a social explosion in the wake of the Party's actions towards the Church, and a marked shift in policy was therefore initiated. A general amnesty and rehabilitation of imprisoned priests and believers was put into action. The Party authorities had not given up their goal of achieving an atheist state, but they began to use less overt methods to bring this about.

Khrushchev's tough methods did not reduce the number of believers. Moreover, it forced a large section of the Church underground, where it was far more dangerous to the system because it was more difficult to detect and to control. In addition, these methods awakened sympathy for believers among a broad swathe of non-religious people. In other words, the what has been called 'the Party's last fight against the Russian church' was lost.

3
'Give Us Decent Homes!'

Ever since the mid-1950s, Soviet propaganda had repeatedly claimed that the Soviet people as a whole, and especially the least well-off section of society, would be able to look forward, within the foreseeable future, to having decent housing. Apartments were being built at an unprecedented rate, but it was still not sufficient to meet people's needs, let alone to fulfil their expectations. Moreover there was a widespread belief that apartments were being distributed not so much according to need, or to people's place in the housing queue, but according to their place in the state and Party hierarchy. All this seems to have contributed significantly to the weakening of the population's trust in the authorities, and thereby to have undermined the authority of the government and Party. The leadership was aware of the political significance of the problem, and their worry over the frustration of citizens, and the increasing openness with which it was expressed, was evident.

A review of the situation carried out in 1961 suggested that in Moscow alone over three million people were living in very poor conditions. They were crammed together in cellars, in ramshackle barracks, in abandoned industrial buildings, in lofts and in so-called colleges. The average living space was around two square metres per resident.[1] Another report shows that the plan for building new housing in 1960 had been under-fulfilled by 354,000 square metres. This meant that 13,629 families, or 49,443 individuals who had been on the waiting list for years, and who had been promised a home at the latest by 1960, had been cheated. Between 1959 and 1960, homes were built for 227,500 families in Moscow, but only 22.3 per cent of those who received apartments had been on the waiting list. The reason for this was that most of the new buildings were reserved for particular ministries, factories and institutions which gave first priority to their own employees, and first and foremost to those in the highest positions. There was thus a striking social inequality in the sharing-out of apartments and building materials. Of the most needy 70 per cent were workers, but they were awarded only 30 per cent of the new housing, while the remaining 30 per cent received around 70 per cent of the newly built apartments. Many more apartments were built for the employees of Gosplan and a number of other ministries and government institutions, than for the workers employed in Moscow's factories. In 1960, 6,000 people from the former group were granted 42,000 square metres of living space, while 56,000 workers received only 27,000 square metres.[2] It is interesting to note that the local authorities (the district and city executive committees of the local soviets, *raispolkom* and *gorispolkom*), who had been given authority to share out all the newly built apartments, and who in 1954 had been told to give first priority to the worst off, were apparently overruled by the ministries and factories, and were therefore unable to do anything to correct the socially unequal division of housing.[3]

   The authorities' attempts to solve the housing problem were made more difficult by a series of organizational and economic failings, which were typical of the so-called planned economy. Not only were the plans seldom fulfilled, but the situation was often still more critical than appeared on the surface. The problem was precisely that very often, on closer inspection, the figures for plan-fulfilment simply didn't hold water. The planned goal, which the building organizations were asked to meet, was expressed in terms of roubles spent on the purchase of building materials. The fact that the given sum had been reached did not, however, mean that the buildings were ready for people to move in. The Ministry of Construction in Moscow could thus produce numerous examples in which building organizations had deliberately paid inflated prices for building materials in order thereby to fulfil their plans as quickly and effectively as possible. Under-fulfilment of the building plans was thus greater in reality than the figures suggested.

Citizens' complaints

The Central Committee of the Communist Party, which was provided by its employees with information about the population's reactions, viewed the housing situation with growing concern. They were well aware that people's realization of the contrast between the Party's promises and the real state of affairs was creating mistrust towards the Party and the government.

From the late 1950s onwards there was a sharp increase in the number of complaints from citizens. In 1960 the KPK received 2,766 collective and personal appeals from Moscow alone, but in the two first months of 1961 the figure had already reached 472. In the same period the Central Committee had received 5,697 complaints, but most of these were addressed to local Soviet Party organs. Thus in 1960 the local administration (*raispolkom*) in the Stalin district received 26,024 letters concerning housing problems, the Proletarskii district authorities received 23,235 such letters and in the Moscow Tsentralnyi district the figure was 18,495. It should be noted that these districts represented only three out of a total of 17 in Moscow, so the total figure must have been considerable.[4] A review of complaints to the local Party in the Stalin district in Moscow showed that the housing problem was what preoccupied the population most. In second place came complaints over Party members' bad behaviour, of which there were 549.[5]

The citizens' complaints were marked by strong dissatisfaction with the overall state of affairs coupled with indignation at the authorities' treatment of individual cases. Sometimes these letters contained long, well-written and very dramatic descriptions of conditions. They suggest that the sender must have had a certain level of education. Others were very brief and clumsily formulated. Often the complaints were collective. Finally, there were a number of examples of complainants who appeared to have taken leave of their senses, but whose cases were also, to a certain extent, taken seriously by KPK workers.

Below we will look in more detail at various examples of citizens' complaints, in order to throw light on how they regarded their situation and what means they used to influence the authorities and promote their cause.

On 21 February 1961 the KPK in Moscow received a complaint from the residents of 13, Mayakovskii Street. They wrote, among other things:

Help the 52 residents in our house who have been unable to penetrate the wall of bureaucracy and the heartlessness of employees in the local administration of the Kiev and Frunze Districts. The situation is that we live in a wooden house which was built way back in the late 18th century and which today is completely unfit to live in. On one side the house is held upright by posts, which are supported by the neighbouring property, but the tilting of the house gets worse all the time. Inside the house everything is propped up; between the walls and the floors huge cracks have appeared. The walls have separated from the ceilings. There have already been six incidents of collapse, where the ceilings fell into the rooms. Because of the decrepit state of the house, it was declared due for demolition, and the residents were promised rehousing by the local administration of the Kiev district back in 1958. In 1959 some of the residents moved, and the rest were put on a waiting list in 1960. In 1960 the administration repeatedly promised that something would happen, but nothing has happened ...

The letter ended as follows:

We would like to hear from the administrations in the Kiev and Frunze Districts why we residents are condemned to live in fear of our house collapsing? You cannot just mock at people who, when they lie down to sleep, do not know whether they will wake up alive, or who, when they go to work, do not know whether they will ever see their families alive and well again.[6]

The complaint is characteristic not only in its open frustration at conditions and at the way the complainants have been treated by the authorities, but also in the strong moral indignation it expresses, which is calculated to provoke a response in those receiving the complaint. The very fact that they drew up and sent the complaint to the KPK tells us that despite everything they must have had some hope that the problem would be solved. Nor was it the Party that the residents were grumbling about, but the bureaucrats of the local soviet. Whether this suggested a clear division in the minds of the complainants between the state and the Party, or merely an awareness of the art of the possible – namely, that it was best to show support for the Party – it is difficult to say; perhaps it was a combination of the two.

A collective appeal to the Central Committee from the residents of two houses on Khodynskaya Street in Moscow, who since 1953 had been complaining about their especially poor housing, was more direct in its criticism. Here the blame is placed not on the bureaucrats, but on the residents' chosen representatives in the District and City Soviets. In the conclusion of the letter the complainants wrote: 'It looks as if what our people's representatives told us before we voted for them the last time was nothing but lies and fraud'.[7]

The residents in House no. 1 (Barracks nos. 1, 2, 3, and 4) on Vtoraya Poklonnaya Street in Moscow's Kiev District wrote to the KPK that they had been driven to the utmost limit of their patience with the authorities. They related how 30 years ago they had come to Moscow as building workers. On their arrival they first built barracks for themselves, and although these were designated as temporary dwellings, by 1961 they were still living there with their families. They were angry that despite numerous promises of housing they had become 'barrack folk.'

The barracks were leaky and damp, and posts had propped up the walls, which had begun to slide out. They lacked even the most basic sanitary facilities, and neither water nor gas had been installed. These conditions meant that there was a high incidence of illness among the residents, especially among children. Such illnesses as rickets and chronic dysentery were common. The electricity often broke down, and the residents had to make do with candles and torches. The letter stated, moreover: 'We have given up struggling with fleas and other insects, because no form of poison works. The constant chaos of our existence leads to anxiety, bitterness and hatred. And this in turn leads to scandals, quarrels and fights.'

For six years the residents had tried to get gas installed, but their request was rejected on the obvious grounds that this would be uneconomic, since the barracks in any case were due shortly to be demolished. Formally there were sufficient reasons why the residents should have been evacuated to other housing. There had been requests from the local administration to the building authorities to move the residents, in which the barracks were described as dangerous to the inhabitants. This demand had been backed up by several newspapers, including *Pravda*, as well as a number of politicians, but none of this had helped.

The frustration was plain:

It was we, ordinary building workers, who elected them. They do whatever they want, impudently and shamelessly fooling us. We have been promised that Barrack no. 4 will be demolished in the second half of 1961, but they won't give us any deadline for when barracks nos. 1, 2 and 3 will go the same way. We get nothing but formal and stalling answers, they're spitting in people's faces. When are we going to see an end to the present mode of handling complaints? When are people going to stop just passing on complaints to the very people that are being complained about? Wouldn't they at the very least come and see how we live? Barrack no. 1 is just about hanging over the precipice. After heavy rain it's liable to collapse over the railway. The ceilings are rotten and fall down on our heads. But this doesn't seem to bother anyone. What they seem to think is that only a hundred people will be smothered, which is just a drop in the ocean compared with two hundred million! Of course we could be mischievous and just saw through the barracks' supporting posts. We however have our workers' conscience, not the conscience of Glavmosstroi. But we could be forced into it! We ask that the Party deal with our appeal, deal with it in an honest Party way. That they get on with the job in the proper Party manner and restore order to the system of sharing out new homes. We know of numerous examples where people with a good Party record have already had their housing conditions improved several times over, even though they were fine to start with, while we have just remained 'barracks people.[8]

This complaint, like the previous one, describes in minute detail the complainants' desperate situation, but it also shows a stronger awareness of the inequalities within Soviet society and a greater and more straightforward disappointment over the fact that the 'barracks people' have not yet got their share of the riches which they themselves have helped to create. It should be noted that, once again, the complaint is not aimed directly at the Party, but Soviet bureaucracy. An attempt is made to forge, with the help of traditional Party rhetoric, an alliance between the complainants and the Party itself. The case should be dealt with in a 'party manner'. The rhetoric clearly has its origins in the struggle of the 1920s and 1930s against bureaucrats, formalists and other harmful elements, but in sharp contrast to this traditional rhetoric the letter also contains a threat that the complainants will take matters into their own hands. Moreover, it demonstrates a clear awareness of the regime's lack of respect for the individual.

In their complaint to the KPK, the residents of No. 20, Vasilevskaya Street in Moscow have frequent recourse to irony – an extreme rarity in the genre. Their miserable barracks stood opposite some new nine-storey blocks which included, among other things, the Czechoslovak embassy and a modern cinema. Since 1957 the authorities had repeatedly promised the residents that the barracks would be demolished and they would be rehoused, but as the residents wrote in their letter: 'The local Soviet administration prefers to let their resolutions remain on paper. Time passes, the buildings collapse, but the administration's promises generously rain down on us from their mountains of abundance.'

There were neither toilets nor running water in the buildings. Previously there had been a communal toilet in the yard, but this had been demolished in connection with the construction of new buildings on the grounds. Thus for two years the residents had been forced to carry out their natural functions in their apartments, then carry the waste out and throw it into deep ditches which had been dug for that purpose close by the buildings. Some of the residents used public toilets, but these lay more than 10 minutes away. There had already been several outbreaks of dysentery. Accidents were frequent. Thus on one occasion in block 27, apartment 14, a cupboard had fallen through the ceiling into a living room. Fortunately there had been nobody home at the time. The stoves were decrepit and leaky. If one was lit on the ground floor, the residents on the first floor were liable to be poisoned.

In 1960 the residents believed their case was at last being taken seriously. A commission declared that the barracks were 95 per cent worn out and therefore unfit for human habitation. They were informed that demolition was imminent. There was great rejoicing, but nothing happened. At some point a new administrative division of the city had come into force, and the barracks came to be located in the Krasnopresnenskii district instead of the Sovietskii. The administration of the former had never heard of the latter's decision and were not inclined in the near future to do anything whatsoever about it.[9]

On 25 February 1961 the KPK received a letter from the locksmith Aleksei Kuznetsov. He apologized for appealing to the Party as a non-Party man himself, but assured the addressee that he was devoted to the Party and had faith in its being the guarantor of justice in society. The appeal was motivated by his desperate living conditions, which he proceeded to describe in detail. In doing so, he also put forward direct political arguments. He noted, for example, that communism had not yet been achieved, and that the division of housing should therefore be carried out in accordance with the individual's productivity. He then described his own significant contribution to Soviet society and argued that he deserved better than the 11 square metres in a tumbledown building which he had to share with his wife and two school-age children. Since 1930 he had worked at various factories in Moscow, where he was first distinguished as a 'shock worker' and subsequently as a Stakhanovite. Most recently he had led a brigade, which for four years running had fulfilled the plan by 160 per cent. Moreover he had served in the Red Army from the very first day of the war till the last. Kuznetsov presents himself as one of the numerous Soviet citizens who had done their duty, but because of their natural reserve and modesty had not been rewarded in accordance with their contribution.

It is notable that Kuznetsov uses the term *'vintik'*, or 'screw', about himself and others like him, and that he no longer wanted to put up with this form of alienation. The letter itself testifies to the fact that he had begun to take matters into his own hands and to identify himself as an individual subject. Indirectly Kuznetsov implies awareness that there were certain people in Soviet society who received a rich share of society's goods without having made the necessary contribution, but this was not the main point. The crucial point for him was that he and others like him should finally be rewarded for their work. Their patience was at an end; they no longer wanted to make do with grand words and promises for the future.

Kuznetsov wrote that he felt ashamed in front of his children, who constantly upbraided him for the fact that their schoolmates not only had more room, but also beds and even a desk to do their homework on. The letter testifies to a certain 'consumer mentality' among the post-war generation. In this case this consumerism had evidently catalysed a dissatisfaction with the social situation among the older generation, who to a great extent had become accustomed to putting up with circumstances.[10]

Another complaint to the KPK was written by the wife in a family. At the beginning of her letter she makes much of enumerating her husband's achievements and sufferings. The reader learns that he had served in the navy during the war, that his ship came under fire and sank, and that for weeks he was drifting around in a rubber boat on the Atlantic before he was rescued by an English ship. Now he had to make do by living with four other members of the family in a nine-square-metre room where the ceiling was held up by posts, and which was often filled with gas from leaky pipes. The children had tuberculosis. She asked the Party to take matters in hand themselves rather than just passing on her letter to the local administration, which, as she put it, merely spat in their faces.

As an example of the local authorities' heartless treatment of citizens, one of the KPK's inspectors described a particular case in his report. It concerned a former officer in the Red Army, Gribkov, who had written no fewer than 30 complaints before anything happened. The inspector quotes extensively from his extremely emotional letter. Gribkov had been wounded four times during the war, his two brothers and a sister had been killed while defending the motherland, the family house had been left in ruins, and his mother had been shot by the Germans. In 1959, after a five-year wait and over 100 hours of voluntary building work, he and his family, which consisted of three persons, received a room in a communal apartment. He had been content with this until the three permanent residents of the apartment turned up. They proved all to be psychiatric patients who were suffering from shell shock and other ailments resulting from the war. Of the building's 156 apartments, this was the only communal apartment. It was only after certain higher Party organs intervened that Gribkov succeeded in being listed for a new place to live.

A comparison of the inspector's report with the particular letter of complaint to which he most often refers – among the many that Gribkov wrote – gives surprising insight into the inspector's own attitude. The report faithfully reproduces the pathetic tone of the letter, but the inspector refrains from mentioning the conclusion, which might otherwise have seemed worthy of commentary. It went as follows: 'It is possible that you are not in a position to help me, but then I'll be forced, and I beg you not to be angry with me, to appeal to comrades Mao and Novotny ... '[11]

We can only speculate on the reasons why the inspector omitted this conclusion, but there is no doubt that it was in Gribkov's interests that he did so. It may be that he was under pressure to find some incriminating material on the particular local authorities, which he had been commissioned to investigate, but this is scarcely likely. After all, as we have seen, there were plenty of cases to choose from. It is more probable that the inspector had been genuinely struck by the case and was waging his own war against the bureaucrats.

What is typical especially of these individual letters is that the complainant gives an intimate account of the family's woes and describes in great detail their hardships and the unjust treatment they have received. The pathos indeed can sometimes seem exaggerated. The reason for the widespread use of this genre of letter was no doubt that Soviet citizens, as we know, had no recourse to ordinary democratic institutions and therefore had no option but to appeal to people's humanity as fellow beings.

Treatment of complaints

An investigation carried out in 1961 into the local authorities' treatment of citizens in the Stalin District of Moscow reveals that letters and complaints were not usually dealt with on time, and if citizens got any response at all it was most often meaningless. The authorities' handling of citizens was badly organized, and it was generally almost impossible to get an interview. The investigation concludes that this treatment was detrimental to people's trust in the Party and government, and that something had to be done about it as soon as possible.

In 1960 the District Soviet had received 11,500 appeals, and by 20 June the following year there had already been 11,443 such appeals. Of the total number of appeals in 1961 only 2,577 had been dealt with, which was considered an alarming degree of negligence. Having learned from their experiences with the local authorities, many citizens had taken to sending their letters and complaints to the central authorities and the newspapers. As a rule these were immediately returned without further ado to the local organizations. The Inspector recommended that these cases should be treated locally. It was not, as he put it, appropriate that they should find their way to the central press.[12]

From the letters, however, one can see that the local authorities took reprisals against those citizens who dared to take action outside the prescribed channels. A carpenter named Chernov from the Stalin District, who together with his wife and three children lived with an aunt in a dark, damp basement apartment measuring 18 square metres, had at last lost patience and written a letter to the newspaper *Izvestiya*. The newspaper sent his complaint back to the local authorities, which reacted by placing him further back in the housing queue. Citizens often justified their action in sending anonymous letters to the KPK on the grounds that they were afraid of being punished by the local authorities.

One of the KPK's inspectors wrote a lively report on how citizens were received both by the local administration and the Party apparatus in the Stalin District. The Chairman of the *raispolkom*, Comrade Tsydilin, spent only one hour per week receiving citizens. People therefore started queuing up from 11 o'clock the previous night. On 18 June one woman, after finishing her evening shift at the factory, joined the queue at 11 o'clock at night. It was only on the following afternoon that she got the chance to present her case.

On the following occasion five people started queuing at midnight. By five in the morning there were 20 in the queue, and by 8 o'clock there were 103. Those waiting had themselves drawn up a list of the order in which they had come, which they handed to the person in charge of reception, Egorova, when she arrived for work. She immediately tore it to pieces, which aroused great indignation, and several threats were made. At 8.30 she began to draw up her own list of 55 people. She responded to the petitioners' protests by declaring briskly that it was she who knew best who needed to have a personal meeting. The Inspector added, as if this were not enough already, that Tsydilin received people without looking into their cases in advance.

The local Party Committee was not much better. The Chairman never prepared himself beforehand for meetings and was therefore obliged constantly to consult his colleagues and other people during each interview, while hundreds of citizens waited outside.[13]

In comparison with the other forms of action described in this book, complaints over housing may seem a rather undramatic and insignificant example of spontaneous social activity. They contained few elements that the political leadership could construe as directly anti-Soviet, but they were nevertheless treated with the utmost seriousness, and all documents relating to such cases are stamped 'confidential' or 'strictly confidential'. There were a number of grounds for this, which testify to the serious political significance of the housing question.

All things considered there was nothing new in the fact that citizens complained about their living conditions, provided these were isolated instances, and so long as the complainants did not go so far as to question the very nature of the system. Such complaints were known also in Stalin's time. What was new was that these kinds of cases were no longer used primarily as a link in the mechanism of repression which was dubbed 'the people's fight against bureaucrats, saboteurs, bourgeois elements or enemies of the people'. Despite a continuing concern to identify the guilty, the important point now was to solve the problem. Alongside his other policies, Khrushchev's housing policy should be seen as an attempt to release some of the steam from the social pressure-cooker, thereby winning citizens' support for the regime and getting them to work. The propaganda about housing for all, and about the imminent advent of communism, helped increase the pressure of expectations; but when, later on, it turned out that Khrushchev's version of socialism could not keep pace with people's expectations either, the political leadership was faced with a serious problem of legitimacy. Complaints over the results of the housing policy offer a good example of this, and they were therefore taken seriously by those in power. The problem became even more acute in the late 1950s and early 1960s as complaints became significantly more widespread. It all led to a growing awareness of the fact that Soviet society was a society of privileges and that communism was slow in coming; and thus a stronger sense of alienation from bureaucracy, Party and state developed.

4
Economic Disobedience

Interpretations

In the late 1950s it appeared that Khrushchev's economic policy was paying off. Growth rates were relatively good; the launch of the first sputnik and Gagarin's subsequent voyage in space seemed to signal that Soviet industry had become technologically advanced. For the first time consumer goods were available in reasonable quantities to ordinary citizens, and there was beginning to be some slow improvement in the desperate housing situation in the cities. Moreover, there had been a series of social reforms regarding pensions, a minimum wage, maternity leave and the like. All these factors contributed to growing optimism among both the political leadership and the population at large. But it was mainly the former who, in the first rush of enthusiasm, went so far as to predict the imminent advent of communism. Among ordinary citizens such enthusiasm was a good deal more muted. Results never quite lived up to promises; and particularly when growth rates began markedly to decline in the second half of Khrushchev's reign, dissatisfaction began to be voiced. The British economist and historian Alec Nove believes that the main reason for this decline lay in the Soviet planned system itself, which, despite all attempts to decentralize the decision-making process and make the system more rational, remained an impediment to economic progress.[1]

The abolition of the market economy meant, among many other things, that the Soviet leadership had to find a substitute for profit as the indicator of economic success. It was a key feature of the planned economy, however, that the leaders never found a method of measurement which was anywhere near so effective. If they chose as their measure the physical output of a factory in terms of weight, the problem arose that, in order to fulfil their production plans, directors would focus on producing the heaviest items possible. The satirical magazine *Krokodil* once carried a story about a factory which had over-fulfilled its plan by producing nails that weighed a ton. This was an extreme caricature of the 'tonnage ideology', but by all accounts it had some basis in reality. If, on the other hand, the income in roubles of a given enterprise were used as the indicator of its success, factories would react by making their products as expensive as possible, using the most costly components for production. This form of measurement also made them reluctant to produce 'banal goods' such as nails and screws, leading to shortages in these areas, which were damaging for other parts of the economy. Another serious by-product of this system was that enterprises also became extremely reluctant to introduce new technology or to experiment with new methods of production, for any such innovation could lead to teething problems and hence to a failure to fulfil the production plans.

The Stalin regime attempted to solve such problems through control and punishment, but there was no economic rationale to the system. Stalin's successors tried instead to apply economic and administrative tools, but this did little to improve the situation. The British historian McCauley believes that, even in the unthinkable event that all the millions of people involved had behaved precisely in accordance with the plans, the system would still have been inefficient, for no conceivable central planning mechanism could anticipate the millions of individual decisions which would have to be taken to get the system to function.[2]

In a striking description, Robert Conquest has characterized Stalinism as: 'a Marxism that depends on holding together by brutal force an economy that would otherwise disintegrate for lack of popular consent.'[3] This aptly sums up the situation of workers who were deprived of any possibility of collectively defending themselves against the unreasonable working and living conditions imposed on them. One of the only ways for them to react was by exploiting their control over their own indi-vidual working practices. Not even the most restrictive labour legislation could prevent the Soviet worker from using every chance to get through the working day as easily as possible. This mechanism of control was made possible, and indeed promoted, by the chronic shortage of material resources available to industry, and not least by the shortage of labour as such. Factory directors and other managers were reluctant to report absenteeism and other violations of work discipline to the authorities because this would worsen their relations with their workforce and thereby lead to even greater problems in recruitment and discipline.

Stalin's successors were aware that productivity was extremely low, and it could be claimed without exaggeration that this was the key point behind Khrushchev's reforms. It was clear to the new political leadership that terror and suppression were no longer an effective means of social control, but the question was what to replace them with. Khrushchev liberalized labour legislation and introduced a number of social benefits with the aim of winning the workers' trust in the system. The reaction of the workers, however, was not so much to improve their output as to use the greater freedoms afforded by the new system to ease their own lot by exploiting still further their control over their own individual working procedures. The problem was that Khrushchev's reforms had not in any way significantly altered the system of the planned economy itself, nor had it changed the relationships between workers, directors and planners which had been established in Stalin's time.

Khrushchev's reforms had no real impact in reducing the loss of man-hours in Soviet factories. The failure or delay of deliveries to the factories, faults in production, poor maintenance of production equipment and so on were a result not just of the bureaucracy inherent in the planned system, but equally of the system's inability to develop adequate forms of incentives and sanctions. Under Khrushchev, workers had even less reason to fear unemployment, and because of the chronic shortage of consumer goods, wages in themselves were not a sufficient incentive to increase productivity. The shortage of labour continued to make it possible for workers to work badly, while forcing managers to obtain as low a production quota as possible. Now that they had won the 'freedom' to work slowly and to produce poor-quality goods, the workers simply reproduced those tendencies in the system which had forced directors to hoard their labour force, thereby maintaining the shortage of labour generally. Against this background Filtzer concludes:

> The individual worker is thereby constantly reproducing the conditions which grant him or her this relative control over the labour process. Having abandoned coercion, being afraid to face the political consequences of reintroducing unemployment, and at the same time proving incapable of providing the population with the genuine political or economic incentives, the Khrushchev regime showed itself unable to break this cycle.'[4]

There is widespread agreement that the collectivization of Soviet agriculture was first and foremost politically motivated. In the first place Stalin wanted by this means to eliminate the so-called *kulaks*, who were considered to be a reactionary class. Second, private agriculture was not in accordance with socialist ideology. What might – by some stretch of the imagination – be described as economic justifications for the process came a poor third to these prior considerations. Collectivization, it was argued, would liberate more labour for the industrial sector, among other things by modernizing management, introducing economies of scale and bringing in mechanization. Finally, collectivization would ensure a flow of revenue from the agricultural sector that could then be invested in industrialization. This would happen through forcing the collectives to sell their produce at low prices. Foodstuffs and raw materials would go to the cities, to industry and to exports. Exports would, among other things, finance the import of machinery and other modern technology.

Considering this abuse of the rural population and the agricultural sector, it is hardly surprising that agriculture under Stalin never lived up to the quotas for production and productivity set out in the five-year plans. What is more surprising, perhaps, is that there was relatively little improvement in these figures even after Stalin's death, when the state put an end to its extreme exploitation of the agricultural sector by significantly raising purchase prices (between 1952 and 1958 average purchase prices tripled, while those for grain and meat increased respectively sevenfold and twelvefold), and later through direct investment. There was, it is true, a certain amount of progress, but it was never proportionate to the investments made, and levels of production and productivity never came anywhere near those of, for example, American agriculture.[5]

From the outset Khrushchev had put great emphasis on the agricultural sector. The following typical statement testifies to the fact that he had chosen a different model of development from that of his predecessors: 'Communist society cannot be built without an abundance of grain, meat, milk, butter, vegetables, and other agricultural products.'[6]

The American researcher Gardner Clark has argued that Khrushchev's agricultural policy 'was eminently successful in raising agricultural output.'[7] In support of his thesis he points to official Soviet figures which show no less than a 50 per cent rise in gross production in the period 1953–58. The author is aware that during the same period considerable capital was expended on agriculture in the form of both investment and land (Kazakhstan and Western Siberia), and that there was very little migration from the countryside during that time. Nevertheless, he maintains that: 'Since agricultural output increased even faster than inputs, total factor productivity, especially labour productivity, increased appreciably.'

Clark is suspiciously uncritical of Soviet statistics, and other evidence (some of which he in fact presents himself) contradicts his evaluation of the impact of Khrushchev's reforms. The most striking piece of evidence is a comparison of the efficiency of farming on an American family-owned farm with that on a Soviet collective. This research was carried out towards the end of Khrushchev's regime, when the reforms could be expected to have taken effect. The figures nevertheless bear witness to an extremely low level of productivity in Soviet agriculture. The farms in question were of roughly comparable size in terms of the area cultivated and livestock kept. Production results were also similar. But whereas the American farm employed only three labourers in addition to the owner and his three sons, 211 workers were employed on the Soviet farm. On the American farm there was one labourer per 14 cows, whereas the ratio in the Soviet Union was two workers per cow. Each American worker cultivated 87 acres, while the Russian worked only three.[8]

Clark argues that this difference can be explained in terms of 'the supervision problem'. In this connection he refers to research by a number of American scholars showing that the nature of agricultural work is such that the individual worker's contribution cannot be controlled in the same way that it can in industry. It is undoubtedly true that there are limits to such control, but Clark omits to mention that one point of Khrushchev's reforms was precisely to introduce greater local Party control over the *kolkhoz* peasants' productivity and the degree to which each *kolkhoz* fulfilled its plan. This control mechanism was supposed to replace the self-interest that lay at the core of the American system of agriculture – and indeed of the Soviet system prior to collectivization; but it was never anything like as effective. Even the most scrupulous control regime could not overcome the peasants' fundamental aversion to the whole collective system. Moreover, the control system itself introduced several sources of error, arising from the very way in which it was organized. Thus Party bosses were judged by the extent to which the *kolkhozes* within their charge fulfilled the plans, and therefore had an interest in exaggerating production figures as much as possible. The system also led them to focus on short-term solutions at the expense of long-term development. This tendency was starkly illustrated, as we have seen, by the fact that valuable breeding cattle were often slaughtered purely in order to fulfil the production plans for meat.

Clark does not believe that the explanation for the problems can be found in the basic incentive system, since in the Soviet Union, no less than in America, this system was based on self-interest. Like the other false claims we have analysed, this mistaken observation rests on an insufficient knowledge of everyday practice in Soviet agriculture. It is true that the individual farm labourer in both the USA and the Soviet Union was paid, for example, for the number of hectares he ploughed in the course of a day. The difference lay in the fact that the American labourer also had an interest in the final result, which meant that, unlike his Russian colleague, he would not be tempted to set his plough merely to work the surface so that he could cover a large area quickly and thereby increase his personal income. This kind of insight can only be obtained by going beyond the official production figures and examining daily practice, as we attempt to do in the following section. The results of such research are not quantifiable, but they do cast doubt on the reliability of the statistics and on the efficacy of Khrushchev's reforms in the agricultural sector.

Victor Perlo, whose assessment of the development of Soviet agriculture after Stalin is generally positive, nevertheless admits that: ' ... the increase in agricultural output has been consistently less than planned, and has obviously fallen far short of keeping pace with the increased resources put at the disposal of agriculture.[9] This is dramatically illustrated by the following figures: between 1960 and 1974 the gross production of Soviet agriculture increased by 50 per cent, while the national income produced in Soviet agriculture increased only 6 per cent. This testifies to the fact that the increased production was based almost exclusively on greater investment of capital and land, rather than on increased productivity. Echoing official Soviet propaganda, Perlo refers to the poor climate as one explanation for this, but nevertheless admits that there must have been 'black holes' into which a great deal of the investment disappeared without trace.

According to the historian G.A.E. Smith Khrushchev's agricultural reforms failed because he was unable to mobilize 'an apathetic and alienated labour force.' This in turn forced the local Party leaders responsible for fulfilling the plans to react to pressure from above in ways that undermined the overall aims of the agricultural policy. Judging from this analysis, one might at first sight expect the author to recommend a return to Stalin's methods of dealing with 'the lazy peasants' by force, but this is not his purpose. On the contrary, he praises Khrushchev for having convinced the political leadership that Stalin's methods were no longer feasible, and that it would be counter-productive to continue exploiting the agricultural sector to the limit by means of political terror. Smith writes that despite their improved situation under Khrushchev, the peasants continued to work inefficiently on *kolkhoz* land, among other things abusing and failing to maintain the increased amount of technical machinery which had been put at their disposal. This failure to work efficiently was due not so much to the peasants' natural laziness as to the system's inability not only to deliver the required level of machinery and fertilizers, but also sufficient building materials and, above all, a sufficient supply of consumer goods to motivate the workers to make a decent contribution.[10] As will be seen in the following my own findings tend to support this last statement. It should, however, be added, that the energy and initiative spared in the state sector blossomed in the private or black sphere of the economy.

Brezhnev continued to pursue Khrushchev's agricultural policies, but was even more generous with investments, including imported fodder. This contributed to a marked improvement in supplies to rural areas, but the increased production never managed to keep pace with investments, and the agricultural sector thus developed into a serious burden on the economy as a whole.

In the pages that follow we will investigate a number of examples of how Khrushchev's reforms were received and managed respectively in industry and in agriculture. Wherever deviations from the Party line or outright resistance were discovered – whether conscious or unconscious, deliberate or not – they were branded and condemned as anti-state or anti-Party activity.

Analysis

In 1948 the Soviet government decided that a factory for manufacturing compressors should be built in the city of Penza. The factory should consist of four departments and, according to the plan, should be built within four years. By 1952, however, only the assembly section had been built. The other departments had not even been started. According to an investigation conducted in 1959, both the local and the central authorities claimed that the factory was ready, and it was therefore included in the socio-economic plan.[11] Thus every year the factory received a plan from the central authorities indicating the number of compressors to be delivered. History does not relate to what extent the plans were fulfilled, but the investigation from 1959 shows that most of the work on those compressors that *did* get produced was actually done elsewhere. One of the 'subcontractors' was located as far away as Ulan Ude, which explains why the factory's outgoings on transport were enormous.

Construction of the factory's foundry had been started in early 1952, but when the KPK's inspector visited the plant in 1959 it was far from being finished. In his report he noted laconically: 'There was not a single person on the construction site.' Of the almost four million roubles which had been designated for building in 1959, only 4 per cent had been used in the course of two months. At the same time he discovered that imported equipment worth three million roubles was standing idle waiting to be installed. The inspector concluded his report with the following remarks: ' ... under these obviously abnormal conditions it was evident from the very beginning that the undertaking would make a loss, and during the period (1952-1959) it had cost the state more than 66 million rubles.'

The local Party leadership was told to intervene as quickly as possible and ensure that the construction was completed. After a certain time they were able to report that responsibility for the actual building had been transferred from one building organization, which had proved to be overworked, to another, and that the workforce had been increased from 50 to 285 men. Several gigantic cranes had also been brought in, and more were promised. It was explained that whereas in the first quarter of 1959 only 1,764,000 roubles out of the 2,687,000 designated for building had been used, in April alone 1,317,000 had been spent. During the first quarter only 180,000 roubles had been spent on the foundry, whereas 370,000 were spent in April alone. Something had therefore been accomplished, but it seems surprising that the central authorities should have been satisfied with this report. Nothing had actually been said about concrete improvements in productivity, let alone about when the factory would be able to start producing with its own resources.

The wretched state of affairs at the compressor factory in Penza led to a wider investigation of other factories in the region. This showed that the general situation in the building and construction sector, and therefore in production, left much to be desired as far as the central authorities were concerned. In the period 1955–59 a total of 4.1 million roubles had been granted to local industries for the purchase of industrial equipment which, at the time of investigation, had still not been put into use. Often the problem was that the buildings were not yet ready for the equipment to be installed. Widespread cheating in the figures issued by factories was noted. Thus in 1958 construction works costing five million roubles were reported to be complete, whereas in fact the buildings were only half finished and the installation of production equipment had not even been started. The managers of another factory succeeded for some years in claiming that the plan for installing new machines had been overfulfilled, while at the same time explaining the factory's low production figures on the grounds that these same machines had not yet been put in place. It was the latter statement which proved to be correct.[12]

A report to the KPK in 1962 concerning the construction of three chemical plants in the Saratov region provides further strong evidence of the almost unbelievable inefficiency of the economy.[13] Construction had been started in 1958 and should have been finished by 1962, but a tour of inspection showed that none of the factories was anywhere near being finished, and that production equipment worth 12 million roubles, imported from Italy and England between 1959 and 1961, was standing idle under the open sky. Poor organization of labour, the shortage of reinforced concrete in early 1961, and the lack of qualified manpower were mentioned as among the most important reasons for the delay in construction. In February 1962 the Council of Ministers, having discovered how slowly construction was proceeding, issued an order for help to be granted in completing the largest of the installa- tions (the Balakovskii works), but even this attempt at prioritizing was useless. The blame was laid on the local economic council, which was responsible for the building. The organization's inability to do any- thing about the mess and confusion at the construction site, and the very low level of discipline at work, came in for particular criticism. The loss of labour time during the first eight months of 1962 was calculated as amounting to 10,000 man-days. Six thousand of these were attributed to truancy and strikes. Despite the constant shortage of building workers, the organization had been forced to fire no fewer than 30 per cent of the workforce on grounds of absenteeism and drinking. This says a good deal about the complex situation which the contractors found themselves in. Moreover, the work was of very low quality, and often had to be redone. One million roubles had been spent on this account.

Following the Council of Ministers' intervention, the workforce was increased from 1,480 to 5,460 men. However, this did not bring about the necessary progress in construction. None of the reports about the progress of the project are explicit about the fact that it was meaning- less simply to focus on whether the number of workers was in accord- ance with the figure stated in the plan, when other parameters had not been fulfilled. In other words, what was the use of increasing the number of workers if there was not sufficient concrete, or if the technical plans were not in order? And what was the point of simply recruiting workers in order to fulfil the plan's figures for the size of the workforce, if the majority of them lacked even the most elementary professional qualifications or were drunkards and troublemakers? And finally, what could be done locally when the equipment that should have been delivered from Soviet factories never turned up? The problems are named singly and in combination, but they are never thought through as an interconnected whole. It could of course have been the case that officials and Party functionaries were unable to see the connections. However, the fact that all the various elements are mentioned in the report indicates that the authors undoubtedly knew better, but on ideological grounds were unable to formulate a more coherent analysis.

The Komsomol was drawn into the attempt to procure manpower, but their efforts were not wholehearted and proved fruitless. The shortage of housing and recreational facilities for the young meant that it was next to impossible to attract qualified personnel. The majority of the young workers were therefore ex-convicts who happened to be travelling through, or who – as the report put it – belonged to the category of people who were simply out for an easy life. An analysis of the number of young people who were respectively hired and fired in the course of the first six months of 1962 shows how serious the problem was. At plant no. 15, 400 workers had been hired and 4,032 fired, at plant no. 2 the figures were respectively 217 and 1,012, and at plant no. 3, 286 and 387. The analysis was presented under the contradictory heading: 'Fluctuations in the workforce in the Komsomol's shock brigades'.[14]

In 1957 Khrushchev had on several occasions appealed to agricultural workers to ensure that the cities were provided with potatoes and vegetables. These appeals were followed up with a series of inspection visits to the *sovkhozes* (state farms) and *kolkhozes* and to the various state purchase organizations, and the authorities were forced to conclude that the situation was far from satisfactory. The reports warned that the shortage of supplies was leading to dissatisfaction among city-dwellers, and that intervention was needed to prevent the situation from becoming critical.[15] The soviets and the local Party organizations were criticized in strong terms for not exercising the necessary control over agricultural production, and *sovkhoz* leaders were charged with anti-state activities.

In 1959 the plan for the supply of potatoes to Moscow was under-fulfilled by no less than 57 per cent. The purchase organizations had paid a number of *sovkhozes* to store potatoes and vegetables for winter use, but an investigation showed that the warehouses were virtually empty. In the autumn a *sovkhoz* in the Moscow region had received payment for 4,080 tonnes of potatoes, but on inspection it turned out that only 2,748 tonnes had been delivered. False documents had been presented to account for the remaining 1,332 tonnes. In 1960 the 'Dawn' *sovkhoz* had received payment for 6,000 tonnes which, according to the information, should have been kept in storage for subsequent supply, but the purchase organization received only about 2,000 tonnes. Another *sovkhoz* had been paid for 3,000 tonnes, but had delivered only about 1,000. It emerged that a couple of thousand tonnes had been used for feeding pigs, 700 tonnes had been sold to a distillery and 447 tonnes were rotting away in pits.[16]

By 1963, despite large-scale investment in the agricultural sector and increased efforts at control and propaganda, there were still problems with the supply of potatoes and vegetables to the cities. On 4 October 1964, less than three years after the adoption of the ambitious Party programme at the 22nd Party Congress in 1961, the Politburo and the Council of Ministers issued a decree concerning supplies. It referred back to a note from Khrushchev which had been sent out approximately one year earlier, and which bore the following long-winded title: 'Concerning the increase in the production of potatoes and vegetables to the full satisfaction of city dwellers' requirements for these products'.[17]

In the wake of the decree a series of reports were sent in to the Central Committee from the regions, which augured ill for the future. Over the past five years in Orenburg the potato harvest had not been sufficient to fulfil the population's needs, and the most recent harvest had been even lower than average. The 'rational needs' of the region's 865,500 inhabitants had been calculated to amount to 86,500 tonnes of potatoes. Urban workers and functionaries themselves had covered one third of this requirement, through produce from their allotments or through purchase from others. The remaining 57,800 tonnes should have been provided by the region's *sovkhozes* and *kolkhozes*, but this was far from being the case. Thus in 1962 they had delivered only 15,305 tonnes, and the shortage of potatoes became chronic. They could not be procured in the shops, and nor could the requirements of hospitals and child-care institutions be met. The special potato and vegetable-growing *kolkhozes*, which had been set up in the region after 1959, had proved a disappointment, since they had contributed only 3 per cent of the harvest. Ineffectual organization and poor discipline at work were cited as the main reasons for these bad results. Finally it was mentioned that the 131 *sovkhozes* and 394 *kolkhozes* which were supposed to have supplied potatoes had prior experience only in producing maize, and this may have been the single most important reason for the problems.[18]

On 21 January 1964 Voronov, the Chairman of the Council of Ministers, presented a draft announcement concerning the supply situation. The draft was based on the reported experiences and suggestions for improvements which had come in from the regions. The first paragraph dealt with the need for the Department of Commerce to be given a larger share of the profits to reinvest in improved equipment, storage facilities and transport. It was also recommended that the state bank should give three-to-five-year loans for building warehouses. The Ministry of Transport was told to ensure that an increased number of refrigerated goods trains were made available, that transportation was speeded up and that the freight wagons were weighed both before departure and on arrival. In addition, the Ministry should make sure that all freight wagons were fitted with hatches and bars, to avoid widespread theft during transportation. The height of the loads in the wagons should be reduced from 1.8 metres to 1.6. It was hoped by this means to prevent large quantities of potatoes from rotting under too great a pressure. Since a large part of the expenses involved in producing vegetables went on heating greenhouses, it was proposed that the currently very low price of energy be increased. This would force producers to economize on energy, but it was also expected that this would lead to greater efficiency in production.[19]

The crisis over potatoes and vegetables demonstrates the distance between the visions outlined in the third Party programme and the reality. Should the country's top leaders really be using energy on something so basic as the production of potatoes? Was it up to them to decide and check the correct height of loads in railway carriages? That they should be required to do so says a great deal about the failure to utilize properly both the social forces – citizens' own initiatives and their ability to regulate themselves – which were made so much of in the Party programme. The core of the problem seems to have been low productivity and lack of organization, not only among farmers, but also in the management of commerce and transport, both in the respective ministeries and, not least, in the overall running of the economy. What was needed, as the report from Orenburg made clear, was a sensible division of labour, so that potato production would be left to those who really understood it, rather than whole regions being commanded to produce potatoes simply because a bottleneck had arisen. Similarly, the objection to old-style practices and the proposal to raise energy prices bear witness to a kind of economic thinking which was bound to prove ineffective within an uneconomic system.

In 1958 the KPK received an appeal from one I. Gusev, who was a member of the *kolkhoz* Krasnyi Putilovets in the Kaliningrad region. He complained that the *kolkhozes* in the region had bought milk and meat from individual *kolkhoz* members and at the *kolkhoz* markets in Leningrad and the Baltic republics, and had then claimed to the authorities that they had produced these products themselves. According to the plan, the dairies in the Krasnokholmskii district should have produced 15,150 tonnes of milk, of which 13,999 tonnes would come from the *kolkhozes* and the rest from individual members. By early December 1958 it was clear to the district authorities that the plan could not be fulfilled, and the first and second secretaries of the local Party had therefore ordered the chairmen of the local *kolkhozes* to buy butter and sell it to the dairies as their own produce. Seventeen *kolkhoz* chairmen drew up false documents to enable trusted individuals to go on 'business trips', that is, to drive around purchasing goods from shops, bases and warehouses and to bring them back to the *kolkhozes*. Some travelled as far as Moscow to make their purchases. Financially all this of course made a loss; but formally speaking the plan was fulfilled. Butter had been purchased in Leningrad for 33 roubles per kilo, which was five roubles over the state purchase price. If one adds in the expenses for transport and accommodation, the total price came to 41 roubles. These kinds of dealings were classified by the KPK as anti-*kolkhoz* and anti-state activities.

In 1961, via a series of anonymous appeals, the attention of the KPK was drawn to the fact that there was widespread 'anti-state activity' within the agricultural sector in the Tyumen region, in the form of fiddling of accounts and other kinds of swindling.[20] It emerged that for a number of years people at every level and in every sector of the region had been deceiving the state. Thus in 1960 several *kolkhoz* and *sovkhoz* chairmen had delivered their figures for the production and sale of grain before the crop had even been harvested. As a result, the accounts indicated several thousand tonnes more grain than had actually been delivered. At the same time it was noted that warehouses managers had cheated the *kolkhozes* of hundreds of tonnes by deliberately faking the moistness of the grain.

In the first half year of 1960 it was revealed that in seven districts there had been widespread fiddling of accounts in connection with the sale of meat to the state. In May 1960 the management of the purchase organization had received 38,000 eggs, but in all three different *sovkhozes* had been issued with receipts for having delivered this quantity.

Industrial enterprises in the region had also cheated in their accounts. In 1960 one factory had raised its gross production figures by 24 million roubles. Realizing that the plan could not be fulfilled by normal means, the director of the factory concerned, which manufactured building materials, had agreed that the production of reinforced concrete and sawdust be recorded as the production of boards and timber. By fiddling the books completely, the factory succeeded in fulfilling the plan by more than 100 per cent, despite the fact that the plan had actually gone by the board and society had been cheated of millions of roubles' worth of building materials, which were already in very short supply. In the report to the KPK it was claimed that the reason for this was that the local authorities had not been sufficiently vigilant, and indeed had sometimes attempted in a straightforward manner to cover up the illegalities.

The inspectors' report to the KPK also implicated the region's two most powerful men, Kosov and Shtyurov – respectively the First and Second Secretaries of the region – in the widespread anti-state activities. In the course of the investigation, moreover, it emerged that these two gentlemen, together with members of the city administration, had initiated the building of a sports centre in Tyumen costing 26 million roubles. Eight months into the construction of the building the central authorities had intervened and ordered that it be stopped, but the order was ignored and the plans for the illegal centre went ahead. The money for the initiative had been illegally appropriated from the region's factories. The inspector also confirmed that Kosov had misused the state's money to set up a special railway carriage with soft couches, armchairs, tables and beds which he used on his journeys around the region.

The central authorities were helped in their investigations by the region's state prosecutor, Ponemarev, who, after making numerous complaints, was apparently very pleased at last to find an ally in his long-lasting but hitherto fruitless campaign against the local authorities. He had repeatedly asked the local Party leadership to put a stop to cheating and swindling in the region, but each time his appeals had been rejected. In 1960 the *Obkom* had received an appeal from an employee at a meat-producing *sovkhoz*, who reported that the accounts of the *sovkhoz* had been grossly manipulated. The *obkom* had appointed an investigating commission, but otherwise, according to Ponemarev, nothing whatsoever had happened. Ponermarev had therefore instituted his own investigation, which revealed that the complaint had been justified. For this initiative he had been given a sharp reprimand by Shtyurov at a meeting of District Party Secretaries and leaders of the local authorities. When he requested the right to reply he was refused permission to speak, and it was decided that an investigating commission should be appointed to determine whether his initiative constituted a breach of Party discipline. Kosov requested the commission to bear in mind the Central Committee's resolution over Beriya who, as was well known, had also committed an offence against Party norms, and ended up being liquidated. This manifestly constituted an attempt to influence the commission's decision.

A few days after the meeting the obviously indomitable Ponemarev again presented the results of his investigation to Kosov. He was turned away with the following blunt words: 'No one has any need of your proofs of fiddling. You must realise that we may find it necessary to take a decision with regard to yourself which will give you something really to complain about.'

Ponemarev was not the only one to speak out against the Party leadership. A former employee in the local administration had also delivered a statement to the KPK. He revealed that he too had on several occasions drawn the local Party's attention to widespread cheating in the region's industries, but each time he had been dismissed. Finally he had written to the Central Committee, but had withdrawn his complaint following threats from the local authorities.

Under pressure from representatives of the central authorities, Kosov was finally obliged to make various admissions. He conceded that it was quite true that there were certain agricultural concerns and other enterprises which, in pursuit of a 'mendacious welfare', had resorted to swindling and deception.

The KPK's inspector concluded his report by saying that anti-state activities had for many years been particularly widespread in the Tyumen region, and that with their indulgence and 'liberal attitudes' Kosov and Shtyurov had been principally responsible for this. In some instances, he maintained, individual local leaders had been charged, but without exception they had found their way back soon afterwards to the Regional Party leadership. Although the inspector appears to have been overwhelmingly on Ponemarev's side, the latter is nevertheless given a reprimand in his conclusion for having instituted an investigation without first getting permission from the Party leadership. It is noteworthy that greater focus is thus put on the formalities than on the substance of the case itself.

The situation in Tyumen may not have been as simple as it appears at first glance. There is no doubt that neither the local Party leadership nor the region's enterprises kept to the law, and in this sense it was reasonable that they should have been charged with anti-state activities. The luxurious railway carriage was also an indication that the First Secretary of the Regional Party had overstepped the mark in terms of personal extravagance. However, it is also possible that Kosov and Shtyurov had turned a blind eye to irregularities with the aim of giving the appearance, at least on paper, that things were functioning properly. Certainly they were under pressure from the central Party leadership to give an impression of growing prosperity. If this was indeed the rationale for the local Party's behaviour – as it may well have been, notwithstanding that they also personally stood to benefit – one can understand their harsh treatment of Ponemarev and others who zealously attempted to throw a spanner in the works.

However that may be, the Tyumen case testifies to the lack of transparency within the planned economy and to administrative and economic disobedience. The state's plans could not be fulfilled, but since the pressure for fulfilment could not simply be repudiated, local leaders tended to turn away and ignore what was happening. At the same time they turned a blind eye to the fact that the main economic players, in their turn, ignored what was going on in their fields of responsibility. The KPK and the Central Committee themselves were no doubt sceptical about the efficacy of the measures they proposed to solve the problem: namely, legal proceedings, increased control and changes of personnel. Kosov and Shtyurov got off with a reprimand.

The archives reveal many instances in which local leaders, in dealing with the population, used methods that were prevalent in Stalin's time, but which were no longer in accordance with the Party line and were therefore deemed anti-state. A particularly serious example of this occurred in the 'Kirov' *kolkhoz* in the Tatar republic in 1962.[21]

A delegation, consisting of one Matveev, the First Secretary of the District Committee of the Party (*raikom*), Kashirin, who represented the militia, and a vet named Melnikov, was sent out to the *kolkhoz*. Their task was to assist the local soviet and the *kolkhoz* management in organizing the purchase of cattle from private individuals, and at the same time, as it was put, to ensure that this process took place in an orderly fashion. However, the peasants were unwilling to sell, and it was only by dint of crude threats and actual violence that the authorities succeeded in forcing them to give up the necessary number of sheep and cattle. An investigation of the case revealed that this was not the first time that these methods had been applied. It was also discovered that the management had forcibly collected taxes from the *kolkhoz* members, using the resulting funds to buy meat, milk and eggs from private producers, and that these goods had then come to figure in the accounts of the region's collective production.

The case led to a sharp reprimand to all the local Party leaders, from regional to village level. The Secretary of the Party organization in Kirov was expelled from the Party for having neglected his propaganda tasks and for having moreover turned a blind eye to the use of illegal methods.

In 1962 the Central Committee had got wind of the fact that local Party departments and soviets had issued orders to local branches of the defence industry to provide them with agricultural machinery and with help in building projects.[22] The "Hammer and Sickle" *kolkhoz* in the Moscow region had thus ordered a milking station and had it delivered. In a statement from the Central Committee these "spontaneous" activities were described as anti-state and damaging to the country, and it was stressed that no highly qualified employee of the defence industry was obliged to carry out work for the agricultural sector. This would cause irreparable damage to the defence of the country, it was claimed, and it showed a fatal misunderstanding to believe that the agricultural sector could succeed by these means in meeting the country's food requirements. Following this condemnation, the Central Committee received a series of appeals from local Party departments, admitting that mistakes had been committed and giving assurances that these had been rectified. Thus the *obkom* in Rostov revealed that in 1962 the defence industry had delivered goods worth a total of 2.5 million roubles. The Mariskii *obkom* reported that the local defence industry plants, 'PO Box 42' and 'PO Box 18' , had immediately been relieved of their existing building commissions for the region's *sovkhozes* and *kolkhozes*. Krasnoyar region meanwhile stated that they would put a stop with immediate effect to an order for pigsties and a feeding station commissioned from 'PO Box 18'.

The case offers an interesting example of how taking an independent local initiative, in an attempt to increase productivity, could lead to charges of anti-state activity. The respective agricultural and military enterprises had no doubt been equally keen on this initiative, and it is not hard to imagine the mutual benefits involved.

The Party sacrificed considerable resources, and in many respects laid its legitimacy on the line, in its attempt to provide the population with meat. Two reports, respectively dated 1956 and 1959 and both stamped 'strictly confidential', revealed that the reality of meat production fell far short of the goal laid out in the plans. As of May 1956, for example, the Russian regions had fulfilled the plan for the delivery of pork only by 43.3 per cent.[23] In 1959 it was noted that neither the Party departments, the soviets nor the agricultural organizations had been able to enforce the rule that the *kolkhozes* and *sovkhozes* could only deliver well-fed and full-weight animals for slaughter. It had been noted that fully 45 per cent of the cattle, and 76 per cent of the sheep that were delivered for slaughter in 1959, were too young and too underweight. If these animals had reached even the minimum weight, the state would have received 30,000 tonnes more meat. Thus in 1959 in the Yaroslav region the state purchase organizations had received 104,000 head of cattle with an average weight of only 199 kg, as opposed to 280 kg the previous year. Altogether there had been as many as 7,900 young cattle which were underweight and exhausted. Meanwhile the 'Red Lighthouse' *sovkhoz* in Rostov had delivered 59 head of cattle with an average weight of only 91 kg.[24]

In collusion with the regional *sovkhoz* management, the directors of three *sovkhozes* in the Ivanovo region had engaged in a special form of economic crime. First, they had received a payment of 775,526 roubles from the meat-purchase organization for the supply of 670 head of cattle. Later the very same day they had bought the cattle back at a price of only 134,653 roubles. By this means they could make it appear that they had fulfilled the supply plans, while at the same time making a good sum of money on the side. It was revealed, moreover, that these transactions had taken place without so much as a single head of cattle leaving any of the *sovkhozes* involved.

In summer 1961 V.K. Ustinov, who was the head of the local department under the Russian Council of Ministers Control Group, sent a comprehensive report concerning agriculture in the Amur region respectively to the Central Committee and the Council of Ministers. He had tried in vain to draw the attention of local Party and government leaders to widespread violations of Party rules and state laws. But no one had wanted to listen to him, and meanwhile economic swindling and other forms of anti-state activity had spread.[25]

In February 1961 Ustinov had tried, again in vain, to get permission to speak at a plenary meeting of the Amur *obkom*, but was denied the right to do so by the Secretary of the *obkom*. The latter did not want anyone to contradict his own contribution, which contained not a single critical remark about the situation in the agricultural sector.

In the introduction to his report Ustinov maintained that, in order to cover up their own laziness and to give the impression that things were going well, many local leaders had resorted to cheating the state through fiddling the accounts and engaging in other forms of anti-state activity. Levels of discipline, he claimed, were extremely low, both with regard to work and to Party and state law. His criticism was directed first and foremost at the leaders at all levels of the Party and state, who had not, in his opinion, done sufficient educational work and had failed to exert the necessary control. On the contrary, laws and resolutions had repeatedly been violated, and they themselves had not kept even to the simplest rules of agricultural management, among other things ignoring all advice from specialists.

To document his thesis, Ustinov presented a series of cases in which so-called *'bestovarnye kvintantsii'* (literally, 'no-product receipts') had been issued. These were receipts issued to suppliers by the purchase organizations – in the absence, however, of any goods supplied. By this means both the suppliers' and the purchasers' plans were fictitiously fulfilled. It was not uncommon, indeed, for the state to award a bonus in such cases for overfulfilment of the plan.

Despite strict orders from the country's political leaders that seed corn should not be sold, reports from various sources indicated that this practice was widespread – not least in the Amur region. Ustinov reported that on a visit to Moscow the leader of the Amur *obkom*, Morozov, had promised to increase the plan for the region's deliveries of grain, knowing full well that this could only be carried out by making inroads on the seed corn supplies.

Ustinov strongly criticized the way in which technical equipment was treated. Thus in April 1960, during the sowing season, fully 252 tractors (9 per cent), 18 per cent of the sowing machines and 20 per cent of ploughs were not ready for use. During the harvest that year, 20 per cent of the 305 combine harvesters were out of commission. These figures, he made clear, were not made apparent in the *kolkhozes'* and *sovkhozes'* own accounts.

In 1961 the Central Committee issued a decree, marked 'secret', concerning conditions in the agricultural sector in the Omsk region. This revealed that there had been widespread anti-state activity in the region in the form of false information about production results. Thus, for example, payment had been made for 2.5 million kg (2,500 tonnes) of grain which the state had never actually received.[26]

One of the many reports which had led to an investigation of the situation, and which became the pretext for the decree, came from N. Rozhdestvenskii, a member of the administration in the regional soviet. He revealed that the last few years had been extremely difficult, because the *obkom* had used all its energy on covering up instances of neglect and deception of the state. In 1959, for example, the Central Committee had been informed that the region had prematurely fulfillled the plan for the supply of grain. The truth was, however, that a significant proportion of this delivery had consisted of seed, and this had meant that in 1960 the *sovkhozes* and *kolkhozes* had not had sufficient quantities of seed for the forthcoming sowing. Requesting the state for increased supplies of seed, on the grounds that they intended to sow a larger area than had been planned had solved this problem. They were granted the amount requested, without in fact extending the area sowed.

In 1959 and 1960 the region's agricultural management had forcibly confiscated large quantities of seed corn from the *kolkhozes*, *sovkhozes* and individuals' private supplies in order to fulfill their plan for supplying the state. This had meant that one in five calves and one in five pigs had died of hunger. In order to cover up this loss, they had purchased 118,600 additional head of cattle, rather than the 2,000 intended to increase the herd.

Rozhdestvenskii's explanation as to how all this could happen without anyone intervening was that, because the members of the central Party leadership had been on such friendly terms with the local leaders, it had been all too easy to pull the wool over their eyes. He revealed that Aristov, who was a member of the Presidium of the Central Committee, had visited the region on several occasions and publicly praised the leaders of the *obkom*. For those who knew better – as most did, according to Rozhdestvenskii – it had been intolerable to watch this mutual backslapping. He told the KPK's inspector: 'All these circumstances meant that criticism and self criticism were banished from the region's Party headquarters to private apartments, where they were stored up under lock and key.'

The local leaders responsible, Koloshchunskii and Ladeishchkov, who were the heads respectively of the *obkom* and the *obispolkom* (the executive committee at district level), were eventually forced under strong pressure to confess. They did so in a letter to the Central Committee, where they excused themselves by saying that they had come up with fictitious production results because they had been afraid to admit that they had not been capable of fulfilling the plans. At the same time they promised to turn over a new leaf. 'We have drawn the necessary conclusions on the basis of these criticisms, and we will let ourselves be guided by N.S. Khrushchev's instructions to strengthen plan discipline. We declare to the Central Committee that in the Omsk Regional Party organization there will in future be no such shameful dealings.'

Despite overwhelming evidence that the reports were correct, the two leaders succeeded in keeping their positions. Although they were subjected to tough criticism at a plenary meeting of the *obkom* in June 1961, and although it was suggested that they should be removed, they were nevertheless re-elected. Instead, one of their most hard-hitting critics, Avdeev, who was a District Party Secretary and one of the most diligent informants to the Central Committee on irregularities in the region, was expelled from the *obkom*.[27]

On 7 February 1961 a meeting was held by the Party Committee in the 'Yakomskii' *sovkhoz*. Ten permanent members and 19 invited guests took part. The reason for the meeting was that the *sovkhoz* had been investigated by the central authorities and, as a consequence, charged with anti-state activities in the form of failing to exercise proper control, cheating and laziness. This had led, it was alleged, to their failing to carry out their obligations with regard to the supply of potatoes and vegetables to Moscow. The situation was all the more serious because this *sovkhoz* was among those which since 1957 had been granted significant extra resources to help it fulfil the plans. At the meeting, members of the *sovkhoz* management responded to these charges. In their view, what was involved was not so much anti-state activities, as the fact that the system itself did not allow for rational economic behaviour. The underlying causes should at any rate by sought outside the *sovkhoz*.

One of the speakers, Egorov, said that the harvest had gone as planned, and that the figures that had been given for the harvest itself and for the storage of produce in the warehouses were correct. The problem was that Moscow had not sent as many trucks as promised, and that the harvested cabbage had therefore lain too long in the fields. Another speaker, V.M. Lyurov, agreed that the problem lay with transportation, which was outside the *sovkhoz*'s sphere of responsibility. He also mentioned, by way of justification, that Moscow had not fulfilled its promise to build proper storehouses, which meant that hundreds of tons of produce had rotted. If the authorities had sent out their representatives in time to look at the harvest and at the conditions for storage, they would have been able to confirm, in his view, that there had not been any fiddling with the figures. He concluded his intervention by saying that the *sovkhoz* management had been made a scapegoat for mistakes that had been committed in Moscow.

Two further speakers also took the view that the transport problem was the reason for the poor results. A man named Kuvshinov said that the *sovkhoz* was frequently told that two to three hundred trucks would be sent. The necessary number of workers was hired and the cabbage harvested, but as a rule far fewer vehicles were sent. The workers were therefore left idle for days on end while they waited for transport, and meanwhile the cabbage was left rotting in the fields. A speaker named Churyakov related how, on a visit to Moscow, he had seen that trucks often stood unloaded for weeks at a time because the Department of Commerce was not geared to receiving so much produce. Often the trucks were obliged to return to the *sovkhoz*.

There is hardly any doubt that up until the late 1950s Khrushchev's reforms had a certain positive effect, but thereafter production was unable to keep up with consumer demand. The political leadership was kept informed of signs of crisis in the economy, and the reports grew steadily more critical, but it was as if the reformers' energy was already used up, and their inherited ideological baggage stymied further initiatives. They started instead to resort to sanctions against economic and political leaders at the central and local level and against workers and peasants who were accused of anti-state activities; but this was like beating the air, because to a large extent the roots of the problem lay in the very nature of the economic and political system. These were the traditional defects of a planned economy, most of which boiled down to the fact that in a system without a money economy and market-determined prices, it was impossible to secure economic efficiency, and to bring the activity of local economic agents into line with the interests of the state and society as a whole.

Who could blame the director of a factory or the chairman of a *sovkhoz* for thinking first of all of himself and of his own local enterprise, rather than of the total socialist economy? To a very large extent, in other words, anti-soviet activity was a product of the system itself, rather than of anti-social elements among the various agents of the economy; though no doubt these existed as well.

5

The 1961 Party Programme

In 1958 the Central Committee set up a working group whose task was to compose a draft for a new Party programme.[1] The group consisted of leading Communists, certain prominent journalists and a number of trusted social researchers from various fields. The work was to be carried out in comfortable surroundings at the Sosny health resort outside Moscow. Until now this place had served as a residence for foreign communists.

The working group was not given *carte blanche* to draw up the programme, but proceeded from a series of guidelines worked out by the Central Committee's bureaucracy, members of the Politburo and Khrushchev personally. The draft programme was approved by a plenum of the Central Committee in 1961. Thereafter, in accordance with the plan, it was made public, and there followed a quite extensive public debate. Local branches of the Party, Party members and ordinary citizens were given the opportunity to discuss and express their opinions of the programme. Suggestions and proposed amendments could be sent to the Central Committee. For this purpose a series of editorial groups had been set up to handle the incoming suggestions and if possible work them into the draft programme. The final draft was approved at a plenum of the Central Committee later that year in October 1961, and was finally passed at the 22nd Party Congress, which took place in the same month. (The two previous programmes had been passed respectively at the Second and Eighth Party Congresses in 1903 and 1919.)

The procedure for working out the programme, not least including the public phases of discussion, was an expression of the Party leadership's attempt to rationalize the process and especially to mobilize Soviet society and thereby win active backing for the Party's policies. When the whole process was over it was calculated that 82 million people had taken part in the discussions. This led Khrushchev to utter the following enthusiastic, but somewhat vague pronouncement: 'The Programme has been unanimously approved by all Communists and by the whole Soviet people.'[2] On the same occasion he said: 'In this programme the people see the bright prospects for their fatherland, and this is what gives them the strength to work. The programme has led to a massive influx of energy and inspired immense creative strength.'

There is no doubt that the process had a mobilizing effect, but Khrushchev exaggerated its significance. His personal popularity was on the wane, because he had been unable to fulfil his promises of better food supplies and better living conditions, and against this background the Programme's promise of the imminent arrival of communism became meaningless. The following popular saying illustrates the mood: 'Khrushchev is a chatterbox – where's all the abundance?' (*'Khrushchev boltun – gde izobilie?'*).

There was, of course, no question of an open and democratic debate about the Party programme. Everything was closely supervised and steered by the Party, which attempted to ensure that the discussions were kept within what they understood as the bounds of socialism. Participants, who were mostly Party members, were in general well aware of what these boundaries were, but despite this their proposals frequently went in directions contrary to the Party's wishes. Below, we shall see some examples of this.

Khrushchev on the draft programme

Khrushchev was very sceptical about the draft programme's formula that work under communism would be the primary need in life, and therefore proposed that the words 'and necessity' be added. He thereby revealed an understandable but nevertheless total lack of understanding of Marx's idea that the transition from capitalism to communism was synonymous with the transition from 'the realm of necessity to that of freedom.' On the same basis he proposed that the communist doctrine 'from each according to his ability, to each according to his needs' be toned down. He believed that people would understand this simply to mean that they could work when they felt like it, and otherwise simply make free use of the wealth of society; and that was certainly not the idea. The true communist society, it was true, was a well-organized, technologically advanced mechanism where there would no longer be a place for laborious physical labour, but this did not mean, according to Khrushchev, that human beings would be redundant in the process of production. He wrote: 'We should not teach people that what we are talking of here is some formless society of animals who can use their time just as they please. We must also talk of duty.'[3] Work and discipline should continue to be given the highest importance; otherwise people would lapse into saying: 'Shall I go to work or to the beach?'[4] Khrushchev took the view that expressions such as 'communist or socialist work' were empty platitudes. The most important things were competition, new technology, new organization and high productivity.

Other members of the Central Committee were also sceptical about the idea of work expressed in the draft programme. One member expressed his view as follows: 'The building of communism requires work and more work, discipline and more discipline.'[5]

The Party leadership had its feet on the ground in this instance, but strictly speaking they were opposing not only the authors of the draft programme but also the classic authors of communist ideology. According to the latter, concepts such as duty and discipline should disappear in a communist society.

Khrushchev was extremely critical of the weighting given in the draft programme to the 'A' and 'B' sectors of the economy. Too much emphasis, in his view, had been put on industrial means of production (the A sector), and he therefore advocated that individual human needs be given first priority. He was well aware that such a proposal would earlier have been deemed a 'Right deviation', but pointed out that conditions had changed. He also wanted concrete mathematical calculations and demonstrations to show that the Soviet population in 1970 would be better provided for than the American, in terms of food and consumer goods. Several members of the Central Committee warned against putting concrete figures on the table. They foresaw protest from the population if the promises were not fulfilled. However, the prominent economist Strumilin, who was one of the authors of the draft programme, supported Khrushchev. A simple projection of the growth rate within both industry and agriculture from 1953 onwards showed, claimed Strumilin, that within the foreseeable future the Soviet Union would be the leading country in the world.[6] Soviet economists were not alone in being optimistic on behalf of the Soviet Union. Many of their Western colleagues were also convinced that growth would continue.[7]

However, Khrushchev was not consistently optimistic. The promise in the draft programme, that within ten years all citizens would have free housing, was in his view too concrete, and he suggested a more cautious formulation. One explanation could be that he was well aware that they were already having difficulty in keeping to their relatively modest plans in the construction sector.

In a speech about the new Party programme delivered to the plenum of the Central Committee in June 1961, Khrushchev gave assurances that all the necessary calculations were in place, and that communism would be achieved within the next 20 years. He stressed that the growth in the population's consumption would be socialism's most important weapon.[8]

There was nothing new in the Soviet leader promising the population that brighter times were on the way, but what was new was that the promises should be accompanied by concrete and perceptible steps in the promised direction. Behind this was a recognition on the part of the political leaders that Stalin's methods were no longer either politically or economically viable, and that the state needed the participation of society as an active player. When the population realized that the Party was unable to keep to its promises, frustration grew and the will to co-operate vanished. It was perhaps because they realized this that leading members of the Central Committee reserved their strongest criticisms for the section of the draft programme that was devoted to the relation between state and society. It was claimed in this section that the Soviet Union had reached a level of development at which force was no longer necessary. The state had become 'the whole people's state', and the time had come now to begin transferring power from the state to society. Decision-making processes should be decentralized, and the engagement, responsibility and productivity of individual citizens would thereby grow. This idea was dressed up with a quotation from Lenin: 'Any need whatsoever for violence against people will disappear, as the people becomes accustomed to upholding the elementary rules of social life without violence and suppression.'[9]

Members of the Central Committee and Khrushchev himself were well aware that this state of affairs in society was not in fact imminent. There were still, it was claimed, a great many antisocial elements, speculators, troublemakers, criminals and hostile agents. They knew very well, moreover, that by no means everyone was working conscientiously and of their own free will.

The debate

Below we will look at some examples of the suggestions which ordinary Party members and citizens sent to the Central Committee in connection with the public phase of debate.

In the period 21–25 August 1961, Working Group 2, which was concerned with political theory, had received 800 suggestions for changes in the programme's theoretical section. However, the working group did not consider that any of these suggestions could be used. There were a number of very long, independently worked out proposals, but these were unacceptable because their authors, it was claimed, did not have sufficient insight into Marxism-Leninism. Other proposals showed that their authors were not entirely in their right minds, while yet others were described as slanderous and anti-soviet. They were all sent back to their respective Party departments or to the KGB.

Judging by the number of commentaries and proposals sent in, the question of personal ownership was greatly on people's minds. The suggestions reveal a widespread awareness that there was considerable social inequality in the country. Some expressed the view that the Party should intensify its struggle against any kind of 'owner-psychology', while others advocated the total abolition of any form of property rights for individuals. Thus the *obkom* in the Penza region sent in a proposal that all communists should immediately get rid of their houses, summer-houses and cars, on the grounds that the means for acquiring these goods could not be earned honestly, and that possession of such things did great damage to the Party's reputation among the population. Another proposal was to forbid trade in houses, summer-houses and cars, since this gave large (unearned) income to members of the privileged layers of society.[10]

Those working in the Central Committee apparatus opposed these attacks on personal property rights. They wanted to stick to the point in the programme that guaranteed the right to personal ownership. They did not in fact disagree in principle with the radical proposals made, but only with the method and time-scale suggested. Thus they wrote that this was a question which was of deep concern to the masses, and that it would therefore be wrong to attempt to resolve it at one stroke. In their view, once society was sufficiently wealthy 'to provide everything for everyone,' concepts such as one's own private summer-house or car would become as absurd as that of one's own private theatre or train.

Like the majority of those who expressed an opinion on this point, one Party member from Moscow endorsed the idea of personal property rights, but his argument differed from that of the Party. In his view, the masses would be unwilling to let go of their property rights. Instead of struggling against this attitude, it would be better to harness it for the purpose of increasing productivity. He warned moreover against taking things too far in this field in order to protect the Soviet Union's reputation among workers in other countries.

In connection with the introduction of the first Five Year Plan, the Party moved away from the experiments of the 1920s which aimed at equal pay for everyone. By the mid-1920s the so-called 'Partmaksimum', whereby Party functionaries could not earn more than an ordinary worker, had been abolished. In the 1930s, similarly, unequal wages were reintroduced among ordinary employees – a policy launched under the slogan 'Away with the equalizers!' Ideologically it was justified on the basis of Karl Marx's words that, under socialism, an individual should be rewarded according to his contribution. This principle was adhered to under Khrushchev, and any tendency towards equalization was opposed. At the same time there was awareness that particular groups within the population were unfairly privileged.

Certain voices among the population could still be heard in favour of unconditional equality, but by far the majority sought only for the most obvious disparities to be removed. Among those who supported the first view was a certain Shukov from Leningrad. He believed that an equal distribution of material goods should immediately be introduced. In his opinion, distribution according to work contribution was unfair.

Two workers from Krasnodar suggested that the total wage fund be divided among the total number of workers, and that everyone should receive an equal wage irrespective of the nature of their work and their position. Others demanded that those who, for one reason or another, were incapable of work, should also have their share. These suggestions were rejected on the grounds that they would lead to a slackening in work discipline and involve the state in very heavy expenses.[11]

Among the second group of indignant citizens was a worker from Magnitogorsk. He writes ironically of the promise made in the programme to reduce disparities in income over the next 20 years: 'They're already getting what they need, so twenty years doesn't seem so bad for them, but the rest of us will have to live with all these shortages.'[12] A worker from Moscow wrote: 'A minister doesn't use fifteen times as much strength as an ordinary engineer, nor does he use 30–40 times as much as a cleaning woman.' He suggested that such wage differentials should be reduced. He was afraid that otherwise popular opinion would develop in an unhealthy direction. The general feeling was already expressed, for example, in the popular joke: 'Why hurry towards communism, when we already have it so good under socialism?'[13]

A certain Sobolov from Vinitsa believed that there were already many millionaires in the country. He proposed that there be not merely an increase in the minimum wage, but a reduction in the incomes of the privileged. This would be in their own best interest, since wealth corrupted people. A lawyer named Kruglov from Sevastopol delivered the following clear and critical analysis of the social situation:

> The division of goods occurs not according to people's work contribution, but according to their place on the hierarchical ladder. A huge difference in wages and a heap of privileges that do not fall within the bounds of the socialist principle of distribution also divide the highest from the lowest today. Why not remove the privileges of the best off and reduce their wages considerably, until it is possible to remove the rift between high and low. All the more so, since the majority will not be able to reach the living standard of the privileged minority within 20 years.[14]

One Gorin from Moscow considered it unacceptable that the elite should have unlimited access to big *dachas*, while an ordinary worker was unable to pay for a wretched shack outside the city limits. A group of workers from Moscow wondered why they should have only 12 days' holiday, while functionaries got 24: 'Where is the logic? We are on the way to communism, where there should be no difference between physical and intellectual work.'[15]

The Central Committee received a collective letter from a group of anonymous doctors in Kharkov. They claimed that Soviet doctors earned seven or eight times less than their colleagues in the USA, and that after 25 years' work they earned no more than skilled workers. This made a mockery of the doctor's high calling: 'Our vocation is to cure the most valuable thing we have in the country – human beings – to repair their health; but we envy those who repair clothes, shoes, furniture and sewage pipes …'.[16]

There appears on the whole to have been no great understanding among the population of the reasons for the draft programme's proposal to reduce working hours. Citizens were obviously nervous that this would lead to a corresponding loss in earnings. One worker from Leningrad wrote that he would prefer to work 12–14 hours a day than to see his family in need. Another wrote that he had never heard a worker complain about the length of the working day, but he had certainly heard complaints about the prices of food and consumer goods. He proposed that the workers should be given permission to use the eighth hour in the working day to exchange and sell goods that they needed.

At a machine factory in Kaluga it was revealed that many of the managers' wives did not work, and indeed did not even take care of their own children. The workers therefore suggested that a paragraph about parasitism should be included in the Party programme. A worker from Moscow took the view that a tough battle should be waged against the 'remnants of private property thinking' among certain citizens, and – notably – that this should happen regardless of the position they occupied in society.

As we have seen, some of the criticisms and suggestions were prompted by a demand for complete equality, but more often what lay behind them was a demand for social justice. Those who were least well off should have better conditions, and this could certainly be effected at the cost of the elite. The letters reveal a high degree of awareness of social inequalities, both as regards income and privileges. The popular wish for better social conditions and greater equality was reflected in the final programme in the form of promises of wages, pensions and sickness benefits for *kolkhoz* workers. The many criticisms and occasional radical proposals directed against the elite led the editorial group to warn that there was a widespread 'unhealthy attitude' among the population, calling for 'aristocratism' among leading Party members to be stamped out.

An awareness of the inequality in Soviet society also found expression in discussion of the concept of work. Many of those who wrote in suggested that the elite members of society should also do their share of heavy and dirty work. A worker named Grebenyuk from Moscow interpreted Marx's idea of the 'all-round developed human being' in a concrete way, to mean that all citizens should have at least two forms of education or training, of which at least one should be directed towards material production.[17]

Many letters concerned the need to strengthen discipline especially in the upbringing of young people, who did not have the right attitude towards work. There were also some suggestions in the direction Khrushchev had feared. Thus Tikhomirov from Moscow felt that there should be a point in the programme saying that the individual should have the right to decide himself whether he wanted to work or not.[18] One engineer suggested that the programme should say: 'In planning their work our engineers should make sure that the minimum materials are used.' Polekhin, from Moscow, wrote: 'I suggest that it be put in the programme that the most effective technological processes should be used in production.' Krupsha, also from Moscow, wrote: 'I suggest that it be written in the programme that production equipment should be used in the most rational manner.'[19] The statements – and there were numerous others of this kind – testify indirectly to the fact that productivity and conscientiousness in economic life left much to be desired.

A certain Kozlov from Moscow suggested that, where a peaceful transition from capitalism to socialism had taken place, all democratic rights should be preserved. The editorial committee instructed him that the take-over of power by the working class involved not merely maintaining the democratic rights of capitalism, but introducing a 'higher form of democracy'. The revisionist Kozlov went a step further and suggested that joint enterprises should be established between western and Soviet firms and that all those who wished should be allowed to leave the Soviet Union. These proposals too were rejected, and Kozlov was informed that 'peaceful coexistence' was a new form of class struggle, not a withdrawal from the class struggle.[20]

A sizeable group of Party functionaries from Moscow put forward the suggestion that all leaders at all levels should be eligible for election only twice, that half the members should be replaced at each election to the local soviets, and that there should be more candidates to choose from. There were demands from many quarters that work foremen and directors should also be elected rather than appointed. Others took the view that it would be a good idea if the director of a firm took personal responsibility not merely for the firms' employees, but also for its economic viability. One Kirilov from Moscow expressed the view that the struggle against the cult of personality should be intensified. In his opinion, too, the concept of 'one-man leadership' had far too prominent a place both in the programme and in the popular consciousness.

From the documents of the working group it is clear that the question of democracy gave rise to many 'unsound proposals' from citizens. Unfortunately the proposals themselves can seldom be found in the archive. Here, however, is one such example: 'What is Soviet democracy? I would like to leave the country, but they won't let me out!'

A Party member from Omsk suggested that the concept of 'elements of capitalist consciousness' should be removed from the Party programme. That kind of thinking belonged to the transitional period, a chapter that was over and done with. People's behaviour and consciousness in the Soviet Union, in his opinion, reflected the real situation in society. In this context one may wonder why the editorial committee did not find it appropriate to comment on his proposal that there should be increased intervention against 'loafers, parasites, speculators, drunkards, bureaucrats, troublemakers, embezzlers and swindlers'.

The debate on the Party programme revealed widespread dissatisfaction with the current state of affairs and resistance to the Party line from both the Right and the Left. The Right wanted to strengthen the role of personal property, while the Left wanted to abolish it entirely. The Right wanted to accept wage differentials, while the Left demanded full and unconditional equality. We have also seen examples of a demand for democratic rights so far-reaching that they would be realized only 25 years later under Gorbachev.

Khrushchev and other political leaders could be reproached for not following the classic texts of Marxism, but no Soviet leader ever perceived this as a problem.

6
Expulsions from the Party

In this chapter we will first examine the statistics on the number of people expelled from the Party and the reasons for their expulsion, then look in more detail at some typical individual cases.

The statistics

At a meeting of the Central Committee held in February 1954 Khrushchev distanced himself from the very restrictive approach to Party membership which had been a feature especially of the late Stalin period. He was particularly concerned about the relatively small proportion of *kolkhoz* workers among Party members (17 per cent in 1956),[1] but he was also keen to see more workers join. The aim was an extension of the Party, so that it could truly come to represent 'the Party of the whole People'.

In 1953 the number of Party members had fallen by 32,000 on the previous year, but by 1954 it had already grown by 92,000, and in 1955 by 166,000. In 1964 no fewer than 879,000 new members had been enrolled, and by mid-1965 the total number had reached 12 million, which represented an increase of 70 per cent since Stalin's death in 1953.[2]

At the 20th Party Congress it was decided that new members should be recruited principally among workers and peasants. This line was pursued until the early 1960s and led to a dramatic change in the social make-up of the Party. In the period from 1955 to 1964 the proportion of workers grew from 30.4 per cent to 45.3 per cent, while the proportion of functionaries fell from 46.2 per cent to 38.6 per cent. The proportion of peasants meanwhile fell from 21.3 per cent to 15.1 per cent.[3] The authorities tried to explain the fall in the proportion of peasants by the fact that the overall number of *kolkhoz* peasants had dropped as a result of their transfer to *sovkhozes*, where they were regarded as workers. It is true that a great many *kolkhoz* peasants changed their status during this period; nevertheless, their numbers were not sufficient to explain the decline in the proportion of peasants among Party members. The truth was that, especially after 1961, fewer kolkhoz peasants applied for membership.[4]

In comparison with Stalin's days, relatively few Party members lost their membership under Khrushchev, which bears out the idea that the Party was now a 'whole people's Party'. In the period 1945–1951 some 600,000 members were expelled.[5] In the years 1958–64 the figures for expulsions were as shown in Table 6.1.[6] Relatively speaking these figures were not very high, but in absolute terms a significant number of people had been deemed for one reason or another not to live up to the ideal of good Soviet citizens.

The historian Thomas Rigby has argued that, after the change of course decided on in 1954, local branches of the Party became very reluctant to throw members out, just as they became relatively uncritical about who should be accepted. The reason for this was that local branches were nervous lest they prove unable to contribute to the expansion of the Party which had been decreed by the central leadership.[7] Rigby's argument is contradicted, however, by the fact that the KPK accepted a great many appeals from Party members who had in fact been thrown out of their local branches. In other words, the central authorities seem to have been less strict than the local Party organizations. Indeed this tendency could be seen already in the period 1937–51. (In 1938, 53,203 appeals were dealt with by the KPK. A total of 20,036 were expelled, while the rest received permission to keep their membership).[8] There appears thus to have been a tradition of local radicalism which was not immediately affected by the change of signals

Table 6.1   Expulsions from the Communist Party, 1958–64

Year	Number of expulsions
1958	53 302
1959	53 456
1960	40 333
1961	n/a*
1962	65163
1963	69 454
1964	68 770

* No figures available for 1961

from above. From Table 6.2 (pp. 88–9) which covers the years 1954–61, it can be seen that there was considerable fluctuation from year to year both in the number of appeals and in their outcome. Throughout the period, however, it is evident that a significant number of expelled members received clemency from the central Party authorities.

What was typical of the period from 1953 to 1964, by contrast, was that relatively few Party members appealed to the KPK over their expulsion. In 1958 the figure was 17.5 per cent and in 1959 8.3 per cent. Of the total number of appeals, 13 per cent and 6 per cent respectively were rejected. Considering that the loss of Party membership frequently also led to the loss of jobs and privileges, it may seem surprising that so few of those expelled, relatively speaking, sought to have the decision reversed. One explanation may be that the great majority of those expelled realized that their offences were such as to make it virtually pointless to seek a review. It was thus only the least serious cases that landed up on the desks of the KPK. Another explanation may be that, when it came to the crunch, Party membership for ordinary workers and peasants was not in fact so crucial. They were not as likely to lose their jobs as functionaries would be, and if they did, there were other jobs to be had. For the same reason, membership of Komsomol was more widespread among students than it was among young workers or peasants.

The statistics from 1956 show that the percentage of workers and peasants among the total number of appellants amounted only to 8.1 per cent and 11.3 per cent respectively, while appeals from functionaries amounted to no fewer than 68.4 per cent. In 1957 the number of workers and peasants among those appealing rose by 0.5 per cent, but overall it was still very limited. Only 1,158 of the 23,163 potential appellants had appealed to the KPK. The Party leadership was aware of this disproportion.[9]

A comparison of those expelled in 1959, in terms both of their social background and of the nature of the offence against Party rules and regulations which had led to their expulsion, indicates that, out of a total of nine social categories, the group consisting of financial administrators, engineers and technicians (*administrativno-khozyaistvennye i inzhenerno-tekhnicheskie rabotniki*) was the most unruly. In second place came functionaries, followed by workers, *kolkhoz* chairmen, KGB officials, soldiers, *kolkhoz* peasants, Party functionaries and students.

That the number of expulsions among KGB officials was relatively high, while that among *kolkhoz* workers was relatively low, may be explained by the fact that greater control was exercised over the former than over the latter group. The fact that the group occupying overall first place consisted of the technicians, financial administrators and engineers is also probably due to the greater interest shown by the organs of control towards this section of the elite. Nevertheless, it was probably true that this group was in fact more unruly than the others. To start with, its members had a relatively high level of education; moreover, they were often pragmatists who were more concerned with carrying out concrete tasks (which they were seldom allowed to complete because of the absurdities of the system) than with the Party's propaganda and golden promises.

This first group, which more or less corresponds to the 'technical intelligentsia', not only took first place as far as the total number of expulsions was concerned; they also 'led the field' in particular offences and reasons for expulsion. Most notable was their predominance in the categories of those who had participated in anti-Party groups or who had taken part in anti-Party discussions. Only a few workers and peasants were accused of these offences. The technicians also led in the categories 'misuse of professional position' and 'violation of work and Party discipline'. More surprising, perhaps, is the fact that they also led the way as far as drunkenness and domestic disputes were concerned. (KGB agents were also well to the fore in these fields).[10]

Table 6.2 (pp. 88–9) shows the grounds on which Party members were expelled, the number who appealed against their expulsion to the KPK, and the number whose expulsion was either confirmed or overturned. As already discussed, not only did few in fact appeal against their expulsion, but in relation to overall membership the total number of those excluded was quite limited.

In 1962, 1963 and 1964 the figures for expulsions were 65,163, 69,454 and 68,770 respectively. Of these, 50 per cent were characterized as expulsions for behaviour incompatible with the high calling of a Communist. In the remaining 50 per cent of cases, members were either expelled for ceasing, for one reason or another, to pay their membership dues or for failing to come to meetings when they were summoned; or they were candidate members who had not been found worthy of full membership.[12] Throughout the period, the figures for openly oppositional behaviour (being a member of an anti-Party group or participating in anti-Party discussions) were small. This testifies to a high degree of unity and discipline. Although the real figure – including those who did not appeal against their expulsion – may well have been higher, it would scarcely challenge this assumption. At the same time, it could certainly be claimed that this form of activity was necessarily limited, since no one could be in doubt as to its consequences. There

Table 6.2 Overview of the number of appeals dealt with by the KPK 1954–61

The number of appeals/the number of confirmed expulsions	1954	1955	1956	1957	1958	1959	1961
Participation in anti-Party groups	105/57	158/133	154/65	229/166	86/76	36/14	16/12
Anti-Party discussions	322/169	232/153	306/91	368/197	243/193	106/57	63/38
Lack of political conviction	446/217	300/137	322/47	329/11	218/162	53/30	57/28
Bad behaviour abroad (after 1959: secret foreign connections)	165/73	50/29	35/7	23/9	97/75	3/3	missing
Violation of socialist law (until 1958: revolutionary law)	170/155	93/78	86/69	170/145	127/112	49/46	38/34
Violation of military discipline	101/81	66/46	80/53	132/105	83/74	26/21	16/11
Violation of Party discipline	718/563	581/446	469/25	2731/448	489/333	417/201	292/155
Suppressing criticism	19/12	11/9	3/1	8/5	33/13	1	11/10
Violation of work discipline	154/134	221/182	143/84	115/74	150/104	40/22	23/14
Violation of kolkhoz statutes	281/192	180/84	92/35	107/46	432/181	25/16	20/13
Wrong information on plan fulfilment figures (ochkovtiratelstvo/pripiska)	41/27	22/9	14/4	25/8	41/24	11/14	32/30
Carelessness at work	1079/771	799/591	584/301	670/413	776/463	309/195	266/185
Misuse of professional position	3315/2795	2194/1862	1578/1170	1968/1587	2083/1571	861/723	800/683
Embezzlement	343/304	282/264	258/218	293/264	252/233	149/129	103/99
Insincerity towards the Party (until 1958: secret past or family connections)	1114/765	552/335	444/181	508/276	887/623	116/72	139/72
Slander	115/113	115/57	101/33	154/110	57/43	81/42	54/33
Non-Party-approved behaviour in private life (byt)/moral corruption	1005/827	897/784	749/528	850/671	736/526	501/393	415/336
Bribery	119/111	103/94	64/49	60/47	85/73	54/50	64/59
Theft	427/404	395/373	312/268	359/320	274/255	272/259	242/229
Drunkenness	1114/999	840/793	704/569	1005/832	832/560	741/645	480/410

Table 6.2 Continued

The number of appeals/the number of confirmed expulsions	1954	1955	1956	1957	1958	1959	1961
Engaging in religious rituals	113/82	104/63	63/35	56/32	127/92	36/32	10/10
Hooliganism	172/141	166/145	104/81	123/93	139/115	85/71	48/40
Speculation	82/74	61/56	48/35	63/55	59/52	55/52	51/45
Criminal behaviour	245/211	130/104	114/91	101/86	121/101	97/84	81/74
Refusal to do agricultural work	315/295	493/388	338/133	198/93	missing	63/19	38/12

Source: TsKhSD, f.6. op.6, d.1.077 (my translation)

was awareness that only a short time ago this kind of activity had meant a camp sentence or immediate execution. If we look at the number of appeals in cases concerning drinking, or giving wrong information about production figures, the small proportion gives rise to speculation as to how effective the Party's control really was. There is a good deal of evidence that these two particular offences were much more widespread than is reflected in the Party's statistics. Economic historians have argued that false information on production figures was more the rule than the exception.

Table 6.2 shows that both the number of appeals made and the number of those rejected decreased significantly in 1959. A report by the KPK on the work of the organization in that year claimed that the spirit of the 20th Party Congress had taken root. This was based on the fact that the total number of appeals dropped from 8,040 in 1957 to 4,691 in 1959. At the same time it was noted that the reasons for expulsions had changed in a positive direction. In 1956 the number of expulsions for anti-Party behaviour had represented 6 per cent of all cases, while in 1959 this had fallen to 4.1 per cent (275). In the same period, the number of those expelled for breaking socialist law or for breaches of state and work discipline had fallen respectively from 142 to 49 and from 936 to 558. All this was interpreted as a sign of greater unity within the Party. At the same time attention was drawn to the fact that local branches of the Party had too frequently had recourse to the highest penalty for Party members. Of the 4,691 cases of expulsion, which the KPK had dealt with in 1959, fully 26.5 per cent of the decisions taken at the local level were overturned by the KPK.[13]

It is by no means certain that these figures indicated any real change in the consciousness and behaviour of Party members, let alone in society as a whole. As we have seen, there were frequently changes in the number of appeals, but not in the number of actual expulsions. This seems to suggest that opposition as such was fairly constant, but that political signals at any given time could have either encouraged or discouraged the tendency of those expelled to appeal.

In the above-mentioned report of 1959 it was noted that the number of cases of drunkenness, hooliganism, and bad behaviour towards women was still too high, despite the Party's increased efforts in this field. In 1957 there had been 1,763 such cases (21 per cent.) In 1959 the figure had fallen to 1,327, but this still represented 28.3 per cent of the total cases. There was a particularly high incidence of this among village schoolteachers, and it was therefore suggested that educational efforts should be strengthened among this group.

Satisfaction was expressed that the campaign against home brewing had been intensified. In 1958 one home brewer had been discovered, whereas in 1959 the figure was 28. This latter piece of information leads us once more to stress that the KPK's statistics should be taken with a pinch of salt. A rise in the number of home brewers apprehended was not necessarily an indication of rising crime, but rather – as the report made explicit – a sign of increased control.

Over a period of 11 months in 1955 the KPK's inspector, Ivanov, kept a careful eye on the way in the which the regional committee (*obkom*) dealt with expulsions in the Kaluga region. During this period the *obkom* had dealt with various expulsions carried out at the *raikom* and *gorkom* (district and city) level. Altogether 348 Party members and 26 candidate members were involved. At the same time, the *obkom* had considered 208 appeals from expelled members of the Party. As far as the appeals were concerned, in 113 cases the *obkom* had confirmed the expulsion, and in 91 cases annulled it. Among those expelled were 17 workers, 24 *kolkhoz* members and 91 functionaries. The grounds for their expulsion ranged from 'violation of Party and work discipline' (41 – of which 37 had refused to do assigned work on collective farms); to 'swindling and theft' (41), 'amoral behaviour' (23), 'hooliganism' (12); 'absenteeism' (2) and 'uneconomic behaviour at the workplace' (8).

Inspector Ivanov was critical of the local Party's work. In his opinion, the reason for the large number in the first category was simply that the wrong people had been selected for agricultural work. One of those expelled, for instance, was an engineer employed on the Moscow-Kiev line who had refused to be transferred to work on a *kolkhoz*. He himself had explained his refusal on the grounds that he had no idea of agricultural work. The KPK subsequently annulled his expulsion. Another example occurred when a certain Petrov, the secretary of the Barkovskii *raikom*, had instructed the head of a local high school to hand in his resignation and seek transfer to work on a *kolkhoz*. When the latter refused to do so on the grounds that he enjoyed his work with young people and had little knowledge of agricultural work, he was expelled from the Party.

Among those in the second category of expulsions were no fewer than 20 *kolkhoz* chairmen who had bought and sold goods without the knowledge of the *kolkhoz* board, and often to their own advantage. The inspector had no objection to these expulsions.

In general Ivanov took the view that the grassroots organizations had been over-zealous in performing their work, but he also found some individual cases in which the local branches had been too slack in investigating new candidates prior to their being accepted as Party members. Here, we will look at a few examples of this, taken from his report.

- In 1954 M.A. Zhirnova had been accepted as a candidate member by the Peremysleskii *rakom*. In March 1955 she was expelled for infanticide and for the theft of 7,645 roubles from the *kolkhoz* where she had been working as an accountant. In this instance the *obkom* had given the *raikom* a reprimand for having been too uncritical in their initial acceptance.
- Also in 1954 I.V. Kozhein, who was a vice state prosecutor, was accepted as a candidate member but expelled later the same year when it turned out that he had four wives. The leaders of the *obkom* felt that the *raikom* could have found this out in advance, had their members taken the task of investigation sufficiently seriously.
- N.V. Fedin was working as a doctor when he was accepted as a member of the Party in 1954. Less than a year later he was thrown out on grounds of immoral behaviour. He had repeatedly beaten his wife and was known to be living with other women.
- In 1955 V.I. Dobromyslov was accepted as a member, but thrown out a few months later for drunkenness and hooliganism. Among other thing he had beaten up the local Party Secretary and stolen from the cash box.[14]

Some individual cases

In the next section, we continue to go behind the statistics and take a closer look at some typical individual cases. There are two categories, drunkenness and embezzlement, which were obviously widespread phenomena and often led to expulsion from the Party.

In 1957 the KPK received a complaint from a certain Borikin from Kemerovo. It stated that for four years the Party department at the factory where he worked had not held a single meeting. According to Borikin, the reason for this was that the Party leaders at the factory did nothing but drink. Thus in October 1957 the Party Secretary, Ivanov, arrived drunk for a meeting. He was in such a bad way that he was unable to read his speech. Following this episode, the *gorkom* intervened and the First Secretary was replaced. But this did little to help. The new Secretary failed to turn up to the first meeting because he had been beaten up during a drinking spree. We learn from Borikin's complaint that not only was the Party organization disintegrating, but the

Komsomol department at the factory was also in crisis, and the workers' club had been closed down.

The KPK sent an inspector to Kemerovo, and after a week's investigations he confirmed that there were grounds for Borikin's complaints about the state of affairs in the local Party. He added that in his opinion there were many other such cases, which simply went unnoticed, and that this did little to strengthen faith in the country's control mechanisms or, in the final analysis, in the Party itself.[15]

An investigation in 1957 into the state of affairs in the local Party in Norilsk showed that, as far as drinking was concerned, the situation was very critical. In 70 per cent of cases this was the main reason for the decline in Party membership in the region over the last few years. The locals maintained, by way of explanation to the KPK's emissaries, that this was due to the fact that during the long polar nights the population had nothing else to do but drink. Until 1956 development in the region had been undertaken through forced labour, and for this reason, the locals claimed, nobody had thought about the workers' free time. It appeared that it was especially the young men who resorted to drinking and, as the report put it, to other inappropriate activities. Even at the city's technical college, which had 1,200 students, there were drinking parties in the dormitories. Sometimes the students would come drunk to class, and fights were frequent.[16]

Expulsions on account of drunken driving were frequently referred to the KPK. One of the more dramatic cases concerned a bus company near Arkhangelsk. It was well known in the area that the drivers often sat and got drunk before they were due to drive off with their passengers. Accidents were frequent, but in 1962 things went seriously wrong. Following a drinking session at one of the drivers' homes, the host wanted to drive his comrades home on one of the company's buses. On the way back the bus fell over a cliff and landed in a river. Eleven people were killed, and the episode led to intervention from the KPK. The driver and the managers of the bus company were subsequently thrown out of the Party.[17]

In 1956 a man named Avdeev, who was born in 1917 and became a member of the Party in 1945, joined with friends to celebrate the completion of a training course in party ideology by throwing a drinking party. In the course of the celebration he got into a brawl with various of the participants and dealt them several hard blows, leading to grievous bodily harm. As a consequence he was later thrown out of the Party. In 1959 he expressed regret at his behaviour in a letter to the Central Committee. The letter was accompanied by a positive reference from his place of work and from the *gorkom*, and led to his being reinstated in the Party.

A certain Gagarin, who was born in 1928, was a worker and had been a member of the Party since 1953. In 1961 the *raikom* gave him a severe reprimand for drunkenness, hooliganism and failure to pay his Party dues. In 1962 he was thrown out of the Party. The grounds for his expulsion were systematic drinking and repeated violations of work and Party discipline. Since he continued to come drunk to work and to stir up trouble, and had repeatedly been caught after beating his wife, he was finally also fired from his job. In 1963 he promised in a letter to the KPK to turn over a new leaf, but he was not found worthy of reinstatement.[18]

A functionary named Zhablitsev, who was born in 1912 and had been a member of the Party since 1941, was expelled in 1953, on the basis of a resolution from the *obkom*, after repeatedly fighting in public with his wife when in a state of intoxication, and for attempting suicide. In the same year the KPK changed the expulsion to a reprimand and a black mark in his Party book. In 1962 this black mark was removed following an appeal from Zhablitsev and his place of work.

A Ukrainian factory worker named Mazur, who was born in 1920 and had been a member of the Party since 1940, was thrown out in 1946 for having made four women pregnant and having drunk so heavily that he had gone blind. When he sought reinstatement in 1962 it was discovered that the Germans had imprisoned him during the war, but he had kept quiet about it. Because of this, neither the local Party nor the KPK wanted to have anything to do with him.[19]

In early 1962 a worker named Kolesnichenko was expelled from the Party for drinking and coarse behaviour towards the factory management and fellow workers. Later that year he appealed against this decision to the KPK, but after a thorough investigation the latter upheld the *raikom*'s resolution. To judge from Kolesnichenko's dossier, there were good grounds for this. In 1952 he had already received a sharp reprimand from the *raikom* for drinking and absenteeism. In 1954 he was given a further reprimand, this time by the *gorkom*. In 1955 he had lost his Party book during a drinking spree, which similarly gave rise to a strong reprimand. Two years later he had been given a warning for systematic drinking and breaches of work discipline. Two years later still, the *obkom* threw him out of the Party for the same reason. When he expressed regret for his behaviour at a meeting with representatives of the *obkom*, and promised to turn over a new leaf, the expulsion was changed to a strong reprimand. But this did little good. In 1961 he repeatedly got drunk and fell asleep at work. The following year, after being elected to the presidium of the local Party, he turned up drunk for a meeting and embarrassed several of the leaders. Later that year, again because of intoxication, he was blamed for an accident at work, which earned him yet another heavy reprimand from the *obkom*. This led to his being fired. At his new job he was caught in a large-scale theft of industrial spirit, which, as the report put it, was to be put to something other than productive use, and this led to his expulsion from the Party. In his appeal to the KPK Kolesnichenko attempted to save his own skin by accusing the director of the factory where he was last employed of various malpractices, including fiddling the books, but this failed to help his cause.[20]

A man named Vlasov, who had been a member of the Party since 1959, was the manager of a canteen until a case was brought against him in 1962. Early that year, he had received a strong reprimand and a warning from the local Party organization for drinking and being a public nuisance. The *raikom* later changed this relatively mild judgement to expulsion from the Party, which was confirmed by the *obkom*. Vlasov's offences consisted in repeatedly getting drunk with various guests in the canteen where he was manager. This frequently led to fights, and when, in the course of one such row, the local policeman, Lomakin, was called in Vlasov refused him access to the premises. As the row continued, a detachment of police was sent in. The leader ordered Vlasov to come with him, but instead the latter threw himself at one of the police officers and dealt him several serious blows. An employee attempted to intervene and received a thrashing himself. The court subsequently sentenced Vlasov conditionally to five years' imprisonment. Not surprisingly, the KPK found him unworthy of being a member of the Party.[21]

In 1959 a certain Naumov, who was born in 1907 and had been a member of the Party since 1937, was the director of a teacher training college. During a study trip to Moscow he had got drunk and behaved improperly with his students. During this drunken spree his Party book got lost. Following this episode the *obkom*, despite his being given a good reference by his colleagues, expelled him from the Party. When he appealed to the KPK in 1962 an investigation was undertaken which showed that in 1949 he had presented a thesis at Leningrad University. This had been failed on grounds of 'gross political errors'. However, he had not informed his place of work of this, and for many years had therefore received too high a salary. On this basis his appeal was turned down.

A *kolkhoz* chairman named Surodkin, who was born in 1912 and had been a member of the Party since 1943, was thrown out of the Party in 1962 on grounds of poor discipline at work and systematic drinking. In the investigators' report it was claimed that: ' ... he gathered the (work) brigade and organized drinking parties, he worked little and drank a lot, and fell ill after these drinking sprees, losing three to four days per week.'

In 1955 an employee of the KPK named Ivanov carried out an investigation into the Party's activities in the town of Kaluga. He was prompted to do so by the fact that, relative to the size of the city, a disproportionately large number of members had been expelled from the Party during that year on grounds of immoral behaviour or trouble-making. A more detailed investigation showed that almost without exception those involved were young men aged between 25 and 35, most of whom had taken the approved route, first as members of the Komsomol and later as participants in the Second World War. Several moreover had acquitted themselves with distinction. Their problems started when the war was over. Instead of resuming their former lives and behaving like good Soviet citizens, many of them began to drink and stir up trouble around the town. The KPK's investigator believed that the sole cause of the trouble was that the Party organization had not taken the problem sufficiently seriously and had therefore failed to set up a rehabilitation programme for the demobilized soldiers. In particular he thought it problematic that more than 30 per cent of cases had not been dealt with by the members' grassroots organization, but exclusively by the *gorkom*. Thus the local Party's close acquaintance with the membership had not been used, and he saw this as a serious pedagogical mistake.

Ivanov's superficial analysis of the reason for the trouble was typical of the way in which the Party publicly attempted to solve problems. It seems implausible that he himself believed that increased propaganda and educational activities would be sufficient to set these hardened young men on the right course again. Their behaviour was doubtless due to their having been, like so many others, brutalized by war – in itself a serious problem enough; but the reason why their behaviour was taken so especially seriously by the Party authorities was that these young people no longer had the same respect for, and fear of, the Party's power that they had had before they were sent to fight.[22]

A certain Davydov, who had been a member of the Party since 1944, worked in the 1960s as the director of a department store. In 1962 he was given a strong reprimand from the local Party committee for selling goods for his own profit. The *gorkom* went further, throwing him out of the Party and demanding that the state trading organization fire him from his post as director. The grounds for his expulsion were that, for a long time, he had sold goods from his store and put the money in his own pocket. It was claimed, moreover, that he was well known for living beyond his means. Among other things he had bought a piano from a restaurant and acquired a refrigerator, a television, a washing machine and four expensive carpets. His wife was charged with having sold one of the carpets to a neighbour at an excessive price. Davydov's expulsion was confirmed by the *obkom*.[23]

A woman named Persina, who was the head of personnel at a factory, was thrown out of the Party in 1962 for having tampered with her mother's work book and had her placed in a higher pension category. It also emerged that her mother had spent three years in prison for theft.[24]

One Bordonosenko, who was the book-keeper at a mining company, was thrown out of the Party in 1962 for having appropriated building materials and workmen to build a house for himself. During the investigation he attempted to put the blame on the director of the mine, who should not have given him permission to do these things. As the chief book-keeper, however, he knew very well that such practices were strictly forbidden.[25]

A *kolkhoz* peasant named Yegorov was thrown out of the Party in 1962 for alleged "behaviour contradicting his high calling as a Communist". He had repeatedly been caught selling tools at the local market, and had used the money to build himself a 90-square-metre *dacha*. He was also known for playing truant from Party meetings and training courses.[26]

In the 1960s a man named Enin was the book-keeper at the Leninskii put *kolkhoz*. In 1962 he was given a strong reprimand from the *kolkhoz* branch of the Party for having fiddled the accounts and appropriated items from the *kolhoz* for himself. Later that year he was thrown out of the Party at the decision of the *raikom*. On investigation it emerged that his behaviour had started to go awry after 10 years' faithful service. He had paid fictitious bills to various organizations and shops and acquired goods for himself from the money paid. For example, he had paid 20 roubles to a hunting store for a trip that had never in fact taken place. Instead, he had collected two pairs of rubber boots and forty hunting cartridges. In April 1961 he had transferred 350 roubles to a wholesale store and acquired 42 cotton overalls that had never gone into the *kolkhoz*'s stores. A month later he had received money from a postal order that had never been put into the *kolkhoz* accounts. In July 1961 he had transferred 67 roubles to a food store in payment for a bill. In reality he had used the money to acquire 30 kg of sausage for himself. Moreover he had removed 640 roubles' worth of building materials from the *kolkhoz* stores. During the investigation against him he refunded this money to the *kolkhoz*. The court sentenced him to three years' imprisonment, but because he had been awarded medals for his war service, had two small children and had never previously been charged, his sentence was halved. During the trial and at Party meetings he admitted only to the sausage deal. The boots and the cartridges had not been for himself, he claimed, but for other named persons among the *kolkhoz* management. The overalls had been given away in exchange for cement for the *kolkhoz*, but this could not be documented.[27]

Drunkenness and alcoholism were mass phenomena throughout Soviet history and may be one of the most obvious negations of the image of the 'new Soviet man'. Among other things this was a reaction to harsh living conditions and professional and political frustrations; thus it may be regarded as a passive departure from the rules of conduct set by the party state. Embezzlement can be interpreted as a more active form of disobedience and a witness to the fact that many citizens were motivated by private gain and not by the Party doctrine.

We have seen that insubordination was quite widespread even among that section of the population that should have been most disciplined, namely members of the Communist Party. The very existence of such insubordination testifies to the fact that the ideology in itself was not attractive enough to be able to gather and mobilize Party members to a sufficient degree. In order to remedy this, a powerful internal training and propaganda apparatus was set up, together with a control mechanism, the KPK, whose purpose was to check up on whether Party members, both in public and in their private life, were living up to 'the high ideals of communism'. In other words, communists, as compared with ordinary Soviet citizens, were subject to an extra layer of external control. The standard form of control, which to a large extent was carried out by Party members themselves, and the control of the controllers, which was carried out among others by the KPK, were necessary in a society that was not held together by values and rules that stemmed from inside, but precisely by external regulations and control.

We have seen how, under Khrushchev, it became a problem for the Party that, judging from the percentage of their appeals against expulsion, ordinary workers and peasants did not see membership of the Party as being as important as did other sections of society. We have seen, furthermore, that there was a marked tendency towards greater harshness among local branches of the Party than at the centre, as far as the frequency of expulsions was concerned. This in itself is an indication of insubordination, since the central Party authorities had decreed that the Party should become more inclusive in its membership.

7
A Scientist Speaks Out

The widespread purge of scientists under Stalin should not in itself be taken as evidence that dissidence was particularly widespread within the scientific community. It was more that, here as elsewhere, people who had the wrong social origins or who had belonged to non-Bolshevik parties were more or less automatically eliminated. Another factor in the purge was the struggle between up-and-coming young scientists and the older generation. In most cases no grounds for removal were given and charges were simply fabricated.[1] There were, however, individual scientists who openly opposed Stalin. Among them was Kapitsa, who refused to participate in the development of the atom bomb – a refusal that cost him his job and his position, though not his life.

De-Stalinization under Khrushchev brought about significant improvements for both the practice of science and scientists themselves. There was an end to persecution on political grounds, and branches of science which had been forbidden under Stalin on ideological grounds were reinstated or established for the first time. Moreover, it was now for the first time possible for scientists to co-operate with colleagues from outside the socialist camp. All this occurred as a result of political pressure, not least from the scientific community itself, which used the new freedoms to good purpose. These also meant that pseudo-scientists, who, under Stalin, had obtained prestigious posts in the scientific world purely by virtue of their political or ideological orthodoxy, were now exposed to criticism. Among those who suffered was Trofim Lysenko, whose inveterate resistance to genetics had done severe damage to biological research in the Soviet Union. He came under attack from the whole of the serious scientific community, including, not least, atomic physicists who recognized with growing alarm the influence of radioactivity on humans, animals and plants and who therefore insisted on the need for genetic research. Lysenko's research into the growing conditions that would yield the best crops fitted neatly with Khrushchev's grandiose plans for the development of agriculture, and for far too long this blinkered him to the actual worthlessness of Lysenko's work. Khrushchev's failure to get rid of Lysenko was among the factors which put him on a collision course with serious scientists. Another area of conflict was the testing of atom bombs. A catastrophe in Chelyabinsk in 1957, when radio-active waste, stored with the utmost carelessness, exploded in the air, exposing a great many people and a large area of land to radiation, evidently led the Soviet Union to discontinue atom-bomb testing in spring 1958, but the tests were resumed later that year. It was characteristic of the time, however, that the decision to resume testing encountered considerable resistance from scientific circles. The well-known physicist Andrei Sakharov, who had been one of the leading scientists in the development of the Soviet atom bomb, publicly expressed his opposition to the tests.

Yet another catastrophe set Khrushchev still further at odds with the technical intelligentsia. Prior to his visit to the USA in 1960, he had ordered the Soviet space authorities to launch a rocket to the moon on the day of his arrival in America. The intention was to demonstrate to the entire world the strength and power of the Soviet Union and of Khrushchev personally, but it ended in disaster. Because of over-hasty work, the rocket exploded in the air, and a number of prominent scientists and military personnel perished. Information about the catastrophe was kept secret, but it nevertheless gave rise to a call from scientists and military circles for freedom from political interference in their activities, which to a certain extent was granted to them.

Political dissent was most widespread at the lower levels of the scientific community. It was for the most part young people who dared to come forward with criticisms and new ideas. Such outspokenness had almost invariably got them into trouble under Stalin, and although the situation changed for the better under Khrushchev, there were instances in which students and younger scientists were arrested under his regime too. This was especially true of the period following the uprising in Hungary. What all those arrested had in common was a desire to take the democratization process further than the framework established at the 20th Party Congress allowed. To begin with these individuals were virtually isolated from their colleagues, the majority of whom were satisfied with the changes that had already been undertaken; and the lack of openness meant that they had very little real contact with the rest of society. However, the situation changed in the early 1960s, when contacts and understanding developed between reformist forces at the top and bottom of the hierarchy. It would be several years before the dissident movement really got going, but a good deal of the groundwork had been laid among scientific circles in the preceding years.[2]

The Landau case

In the following we will examine in detail a KGB report from 1956 on the world-famous physicist, Lev Davydovich Landau 1908–68); but first a few words should be said on his biography. In 1938 he came under the searchlight of the secret police and was arrested. A Western source relates that he was sentenced to 10 years in prison, but does not go into detail on the background to the case. Another Western source claims that the reason for his arrest was a campaign against scientists of Jewish origin, but there is no evidence for this. As we shall see, the KGB report gives another and more detailed explanation for the arrest.

Landau was fortunate that Peter Kapitsa, who was the head of the Institute of Problems of Physics where he was employed, had both sufficient influence and enough personal courage to go directly to Molotov and Stalin and intervene on his behalf. Kapitsa was threatening to resign from the Institute and from his other positions in the scientific world unless Landau was immediately released. The reason for the success of the intervention was that he was internationally renowned and that he led a number of scientific projects in the field of nuclear physics which were given high priority by the political leadership.

A former colleague has suggested that many of Landau's immediate circle in the 1950s were politically engaged and critically orientated. In his circumspect account he gives no direct indication of how far their critique extended beyond Khrushchev's critique of Stalinism, but judging by the KGB-report it was significant.[3] Landau received several Soviet state prizes for his work, together with three Orders of Lenin and two other orders, including 'Hero of Socialist Labour' (1954). In 1962 he was awarded the Nobel Prize for physics. In the same year, however, his career was cut short when he was badly injured in a road accident.

The KGB report on Landau was sent to the Central Committee on the orders of V.A. Kirillin on 20 December 1956. The leader of the KGB's first special department, Ivanov, signed the document, which was marked 'strictly confidential'. It represents a summary of the extensive materials relating to the scientist, and consists of reports from agents and informers close to him and transcriptions from his bugged apartment and telephone. After the collapse of the Party state in 1991, Landau's dossier ended up, like other sensitive documents, in the so-called Presidential Archive, to which researchers have only very limited access. Along with many other documents that were compromising to the Communist Party, however, it was released in connection with the trial of the Party in 1991.

The report to the Central Committee contains additional biographical data which were significant in the Soviet context.[4] We learn that Landau was not a Party member and was of Jewish origin, and that his father was arrested in 1930. The charge against the latter was that he had allegedly been wilfully negligent at work. The son was alleged subsequently to have tried to conceal this circumstance. The imprisonment of the young Landau in the same year was for participation in an anti-Soviet group. As we already know, he was released a year later, which was very unusual in such cases. The grounds for his release, according to the KGB's documents, were that he was a great scientist. This suggests that Kapitsa's and also Niels Bohr's interventions had indeed played a role.

Politically Landau was described as extremely anti-Soviet. He was hostile in his attitude to 'the whole of Soviet reality' and described himself as an academic slave. He was alleged in this connection to have made, in the period 1947–48, a number of anti-Soviet statements to the effect that there was no scientific freedom in the Soviet Union, and that science was governed by incompetent 'locksmiths, carpenters and joiners'. On numerous occasions, apparently, he expressed the view that patriotism had made Soviet science provincial, and that science, the press and literature alike had prostituted themselves. He himself could not have cared less where a particular discovery was made, and he disdained to take part in the foolish discussion of one country's scientific superiority over another's.

According to the report, Landau apparently stated in 1952 that he wished to be as little involved as possible in work on the Soviet atombomb. On the same occasion he said that anyone who wished to live a happy life should keep as far away from the state's assignments as possible – especially from the Soviet state's, because it was built entirely on suppression. In 1953 he wrote a letter to a colleague in which he expressed the view that, had he not been a Jew, it would not have been necessary for him to have become involved in special assignments, but only in science. This was undoubtedly a reference to the development of the Soviet atom-bomb. He stressed that his involvement happened only because he had felt forced into it and not, as the friend had hinted, that he had any wish whatsoever to work for the good of the fatherland.

Thus Landau made no attempt to conceal that he was deeply dissatisfied with the political control of science, and that he had no wish to submit to the rigid patriotism imposed on Soviet citizens after the war. His reluctance to co-operate in the atom-bomb project may have been inspired by the fact that his mentor and friend Kapitsa had already, in 1946, refused to participate in the development of the bomb, and was therefore removed by Stalin from his top position in the Academy of Sciences' Institute for the Study of Physics. He was however reinstated in 1955 after Stalin's death.

The report discusses at length Landau's evaluation of the uprising in Hungary and the subsequent Soviet invasion in 1956. He dismissed the propaganda in the Soviet media which claimed that the uprising had been instigated by a clique of bourgeois and counter-revolutionary elements acting against the interests of the Hungarian people. He believed, on the contrary, that this was a revolution involving the whole of the Hungarian people, and that the working class did not take a different stance from the rest of the population. He saw the uprising as the people's rebellion against a small Hungarian elite, which was able to hold on to power only because it was supported by the criminal Soviet government. Janos Kadar was aptly described as the Soviet Union's puppet. Landau is alleged to have expressed the hope, in one conversation, that the uprising would extend to Czechoslovakia.

On 11 November 1956 Landau is alleged to have said, in conversation with an unnamed woman in her apartment, that the rebels in Hungary had not committed a single atrocity. Obviously they had done so as regards members of the KGB, but he took the view that they were amply justified in this. He saw the uprising as a decisive clash with communist ideology itself: 'Our people are literally waist-deep in blood. What the Hungarians have done is a magnificent achievement. They are the first to have delivered a death blow to the jesuitical ideas of our time. And what a blow!'

In several conversations with friends Landau expressed his view that the Communist Party was a fascist party, which had full control over the power of the state. In a conversation in his apartment concerning what Lenin would have said to the invasion of Hungary, he declared that fascist elements had been there from the moment the communists took power. As evidence of this he cited the brutal suppression of the uprising in Kronstadt in 1921. In his view, power had been concentrated in the hands of the Party during the first months after October. This was no accident or mistake, he alleged, but the very idea of the revolution. On 12 January 1956, in a conversation with Shalnikov, who was a member of the Academy of Sciences, Landau repeated that the Soviet system was a fascist system, and he added that he did not believe that it would ever of its own accord develop into a decent system. On the same occasion he is reported to have characterized the regime as follows: 'How can one believe in this government? Who believes in executioners? It is disgraceful. They are executioners, beastly executioners.'

At the beginning of 1957 Landau is thought to have changed his view of the possibilities for change. In a conversation with one of the KGB's agents, he is reported to have said:

> Just think. Now a possibility has opened up that I couldn't have imagined! A possibility for revolution in this country. Only a year ago it was laughable to think of a revolution taking place here. That is no longer the case. It will happen, it's no longer an absurd thought.

It is not clear from the documents what had made him change his mind, and what kind of revolution he imagined. Perhaps this statement was made under the impression of growing popular dissatisfaction with Khrushchev's regime.

Landau reportedly spent most of his time at home, listening to western propaganda broadcasts and spreading news among his many guests. In addition he supposedly spent a lot of time discussing his intimate relationships with various women. The report in various places emphasizes his loose style of life, but the writer's ill-concealed indignation reaches its apotheosis at the end, where it is related that bugging of the couple's bedroom had revealed that Landau openly discussed his mistresses with his wife.

It cannot be ruled out that the KGB's informers may have added things to their reports on Landau's behaviour, or perhaps straightforwardly invented statements and conversations. There was great temptation to do so, for the worse the situation could be depicted, the more meaningful their own work became in the eyes of their employers. The same goes for the overall summary of the agents' reports. In addition, the KGB may have felt it necessary to make an extra effort in order to legitimize its own work against the background of the new times which had been ushered in at the 20th Party Congress.

There is therefore reason to treat the source with some caution, but there are no grounds for believing that the report was pure fabrication.

At the very least, it bears witness to the presence of radical social criticism among the technical intelligentsia in the 1940s and 50s. There is no simple explanation for this, but one can imagine that this section of the elite ran into so many absurdities in their professional practice that they were likely to develop a critical attitude towards the system. Landau himself mentions his experience of seeing unqualified communists attempting to direct scientific research. It is also a fact that the technical intelligentsia were subjected to fewer ideological purges than the other branches of the academic establishment, in part because they were not concerned with ideology, and in part because co-operation with the 'bourgeois specialists' was so important that those in power were inclined to turn a blind eye not only to cases of disobedience, but also to dissident political attitudes. This meant that these critical elements remained in this milieu, and that fear was perhaps not so widespread as in other places.

8
Uprisings in the Camps

Stalin's death in March 1953, and the removal later that year of the dreaded leader of the secret police, Beria, gave people hope and even expectation of a slackening in the state's iron grip of terror over society. This applied not least to the many thousands of prisoners in the camps. To an even greater degree than their fellow countrymen on the other side of the barbed wire, they had experienced the injustice and violence of the system. Their situation moreover meant that they did not have so much to lose.

On 27 March 1953 a widespread amnesty for prisoners in the camps was introduced. According to Soviet figures, the GULAG system at that time consisted of 146 work and reform camps, 687 work and reform colonies and 52 transit prisons with a total of 2,237,961 prisoners. In addition there were 10 'special camps' with 210,000 prisoners.[1] The latter category, which was established in 1948 on Stalin's initiative, was designated for those dubbed especially dangerous prisoners, who had been convicted of 'anti-Soviet activities'. This concept was extremely vague and covered a large range of activities, from espionage and terrorism or sabotage, through membership of various political or national groups, to simply telling political jokes. Prisoners in these camps were subjected to particularly severe conditions. They had to carry out physical labour ten hours a day, they were granted only 1.6 square meters of space in the barracks each, there was no medicine and no medical help available, they had no chance to earn a reduction in their sentence, and after serving their punishment in the camps they were sent into exile in distant corners of the empire. The original plan in 1948 had been to set up five such camps for 100,000 prisoners. However, the need proved greater, for by 1952 12 such camps had been established, and the number of prisoners was more than double the number planned.[2]

Under a decree of the Ministry of the Interior (MVD) of 31 December 1948 a special 'strict regime' section was set up in the ordinary camps. The aim was to strengthen discipline and stamp out criminal activities. Prisoners who consistently broke the camp rules or refused to submit to the regime of re-education in the ordinary camps were put under this regime.

It was no coincidence that the establishment of the special camps and the introduction of the special-regime sections in the ordinary camps occurred in 1948. After the war a large number of Soviet soldiers who had been German prisoners of war were sent to the camps, alongside people who had actively resisted the Soviet regime, those who had co-operated with the occupying German forces and those who were merely suspected of having done so. Many of these, hardened by their experience of war, were not so easy to order around as the ordinary prisoners.

Almost without exception, the large-scale amnesty applied only to short-term prisoners and therefore did not include prisoners in the special camps, of whom the majority were so-called political prisoners. This was of course a great disappointment to those affected, and, influenced by developments in the rest of society, they refused to accept this arbitrary diktat, and began to express various forms of protest and resistance. All kinds of action were reported, ranging from spontaneous protests on the part of individual prisoners to organized acts of disobedience, which gradually developed into uprisings and violent confrontations with the regime.

In 1954 the special camps were reorganized into ordinary work and reform camps. This change should be seen as part of the general process of modernizing the whole of the Soviet system, and may be regarded as a result of a mixture of pressure from below, and of recognition on the part of the political leadership that it was essential to change the state's methods of control and to make them more effective. However, the reorganization did not take place overnight. An investigation of conditions in a camp one year later showed that the old routines and customary forms of behaviour between the camp management, the guards and the prisoners remained unchanged. For example the prisoners were still not called by name, as prescribed in the new regulations, but by their prison numbers. In 1956, with the aim of bringing about more far-reaching changes in camp conditions, the Central Committee undertook to investigate the whole Soviet penal system, including the MVD's camps and prisons.

In comparison with the figures for Western countries, the number of prisoners in Soviet jails and camps throughout the Soviet Union's history had been extremely high. The reason was not that Soviet citizens were by nature more prone to criminal behaviour than people elsewhere, but that the law and legal practice were much stricter and, in particular, a great many activities or forms of behaviour which would be regarded as normal in Western societies were considered criminal in the Soviet Union. Criticizing the government and living conditions, or engaging in private trade, were just some of the actions that could lead to Soviet citizens being sentenced to long terms in prison or camp. Another reason for the high numbers was that the state had an interest in employing prisoners to carry out the kinds of work that no one would do voluntarily. Besides, the advantage with prisoners was that their work was basically unpaid.[3]

Soviet prisoners may thus be treated as a special form of underclass in the Soviet Union which at various times either expanded or diminished, depending not on the extent of criminality, but on the state's need for cheap labour.[4] It is well known that mass arrests were carried out during the process of industrialization in the 1930s and in connection with the reconstruction of the Soviet Union following the Second World War. There had been uprisings in the camps under Stalin, but it was only after his death in 1953, and especially after the removal of Beria, that a belief in the possibility of change began to spread in the camps as it had in the rest of society. Solzhenitsyn writes that it was a hard blow for the camp managers to have to remove the portraits of the 'criminal' Beria from their offices, and a feeling of insecurity spread among them and among the camp staff generally. Following Beria's death there was an increase in the number of instances of guards shooting prisoners. This has been explained as a result of nervousness among the guards and a desire to demonstrate how much they were needed.[5] The immediate pretext for the acts of organized disobedience and other forms of protest in the camps in 1953–54 was in fact the shooting of prisoners. The fellow prisoners of those killed called for the guilty to be charged. Additional demands included a reduction in sentences, a relaxation of discipline and other changes that would ease the prisoners' existence. In a camp in Vorkuta in 1953 calls were made for the Universal Declaration of Human Rights to be observed.

Until the mid-1950s protest actions in the camps were typically peaceful and organized. Strike committees were formed, demands formulated, and negotiations carried out with the local camp management or with envoys from Moscow. This civilized behaviour on the part of the prisoners can be explained by the fact that the great majority were ordinary Soviet citizens. The proportion of such prisoners fell after the mass releases of 1956–57, and this may explain why the uprisings thereafter became more violent.[6] Of the 21 reported uprisings in the period 1953–83, ten cases were mentioned in which there had been an armed attack by the authorities, with prisoners wounded or killed in consequence. Five such instances occurred under Khrushchev, but in four of these cases there had been no violence on the part of the prisoners. In the case of the fifth, the prisoners had occupied part of the camp grounds, but there were no resulting deaths among the guards. Under Brezhnev there were likewise five reported cases of shooting, but in three of these instances it was recorded that there had been violent attacks by the prisoners, including the murder of guards and soldiers.[7]

The authors of the report on the 21 uprisings, which was written in the early 1980s, say that their material is incomplete, and that the real figure was probably much higher. One can imagine, in particular, that there were a great many more minor episodes in which the problem was solved locally without calling in help or reinforcement from Moscow. Boris Weil, who today lives in Denmark, describes for example how he took part in a strike in a camp in 1958. It arose because some of the guards had beaten up a Ukrainian prisoner. However, the camp commander succeeded in putting a stop to the strike by threatening that the prisoners would be shot from the camp watchtower if they did not go to work.

The uprising in Kargapolskii Labour and Reform Camp, 1953

The Kargapolskii Labour and Reform Camp was a so-called forest camp located in the Arkhangelsk region. In addition to doing forestry work, the prisoners were employed in building a railway for transporting prisoners and timber. The management had its headquarters at the district centre of Ertsevo. The camp was divided into 30 sections which were spread out over a very large area, and each section had a railway connection to Ertsevo. The 16th section, on which we will focus here, was located at the Chernaya railway station, 42 km from the camp headquarters. This section was further divided into two sub-sections, one with an ordinary and one with a strict regime. In 1953 there were 325 prisoners in the strict-regime section, and 403 in the ordinary regime. The strict-regime section had been set up in 1952, by dividing the camp into two with two wooden barriers five metres apart. Between the two barriers a so-called firing zone was established. These arrangements did not however prevent the prisoners from the two sections communicating with one another. The camp management was aware that such communication was not in accordance with the rules and appealed several times to the GULAG management on this point. At the same time they took the opportunity to complain that the staff accommodation was of a very poor standard.

In August 1953 a mainly anonymous group of prisoners, included one named Utkin, complained to the authorities about conditions in the camp. In May they had organized a hunger strike, which had immediately been forcibly stopped by the camp management. The KPK sent a delegation to the camp to investigate the prisoners' complaints. The delegation consisted of one Gulyaev, who was an employee of the KPK; a representative of the USSR's state procuracy named Makushin; a representative of the Ministry of Justice, and the head of the administration in Arkhangelsk obkom, Markov. After a thorough investigation of conditions, which included talks with both prisoners and guards, together with the camp management and even the head of the GULAG administration, a report to the leader of the KPK, M.F. Shkiryatov, was drawn up. The report was very critical and resulted directly in the sacking and prosecution of several of the camp managers.[8] Thus the prisoners won, but without the KPK's intervention the hunger strike would hardly have succeeded in achieving anything except the normal sequence of events before the information went beyond the confines of the camp system: namely, beatings and the removal of the prisoners to the punishment cells and prison.

On 30 May the same year the kitchen staff in Section 16 received a barrel of rotten fish, which was the immediate reason why the prisoners went on hunger strike the following day. In the report from the KPK's Inspector it was claimed that the initiative had come from a group of bandits, but this does not tally with the information that all 320 prisoners rallied to the action, and it assorts oddly with the main conclusion of the report, which states that the prisoners were correct in their criticism of conditions.

In addition to the bad food, the prisoners cited as reasons for their hunger strike the non-payment of wages, rough treatment by the guards and unjustified transfers to the strict-regime section. Despite the hunger strike the prisoners decided to go to work as usual but were prevented on the grounds that hunger strikers could not be put to work.

On the initiative of the head of the camp, Silantev, a doctor was sent out to the camp on 31 May to check the fish. He admitted that it was bad, and having been assured that it had not been, and would not be, used in their food, he reported this to the prisoners. The prisoners however refused to break off their strike, which confirms that the food had only been the immediate pretext for it. Next Silantev sent out his deputy, Colonel Nosov. The latter reported back that he could understand the prisoners' complaints, and he asked his boss to come and see for himself. The following day Nosov and the camp's state prosecutor, Yakovlev, set out for Section 16. Here they realized that there were a number of things wrong. They therefore promised the prisoners that they would attend to their demands and take measures against those guards who had broken the rules. They also promised to grant the prisoners' wish that a commission be summoned from Moscow. On returning to the camp headquarters Silantev rang Dolgikh, the head of the GULAG, in Moscow, requesting him to send a representative to the camp. The latter however told him that he had no one available to do this, since all his staff was engaged in the amnesty cases in other camps. He therefore asked Silantev to solve the problem himself and to be responsive to the prisoners' demands. If this brought no result, he would have to look into removing the trouble-makers. Silantev was also told that physical force could be employed only if it was strictly necessary, but that weapons were on no account to be used.

On 6 June Silantev summoned his subordinates. These consisted of the head of the camp guards, Ruzhinkov, the chief of staff, Glebov, the vice-head of the disciplinary department and Glazunov, who was the head of the political department. Together with 120 soldiers and guards they set out for Section 16. Silantev's second-in-command, Nosov, was already there, as was the head of Section 16. The delegation briefly set out their plan for how the strike could be stopped. The starting point was that all the prisoners should be taken out of the barracks, whereupon the instigators of the strike should be segregated from the rest. The GULAG management as the one customarily used in such cases had recommended this method. This indicates that strikes of this kind were not an uncommon occurence.

Silantev took the initiative and suggested that Nosov should lead the men who were to force their way into the barracks and get the prisoners out, but the latter declined to do this. Another officer, Pavlinov, was then proposed. He refused on the grounds that the prisoners were already angry with him because it was known that he was responsible for problems with wage payments. The choice next fell on the head of Section 16, Chernov, who willingly undertook the task. The KPK's emissary noted in his report that Chernov was a bad choice because he too was unpopular among the prisoners. Chernov got 50 men to assist him. In accordance with the message he had received from his superiors in Moscow, Silantev told Chernov that physical force could be used only if the prisoners refused to come out of their own accord, and that under no circumstances could weapons be employed. The guards were given 40 pairs of handcuffs, but no guns. In the event, the shot that was fired came from one of the officers participating, whose handgun had not been withdrawn.

The author of the report described what happened and stressed that Silantev had a duty to lead the action himself, but that he retreated from taking responsibility when he realised that there could be violent resistance.

On entering, together with his men, the first section of the barracks, which held 50 prisoners, Chernov ordered the latter to gather their possessions and leave. This they refused to do, and a great row broke out, with the prisoners reiterating their demand for a commission from Moscow. Chernov informed them that physical force would be used if they did not come out of their own accord. The guards then immediately attempted to put the prisoners in handcuffs, but the latter resisted, and fighting and uproar ensued. The same scene was repeated in the other five sub-sections of the camp. After the prisoners had been led out of the camp, they were given food and medical assistance. Fifty-three were identified as instigators of the hunger strike and segregated accordingly. The rest were sent back to the barracks. That the choice of the so-called instigators was more or less arbitrary is clear from the fact that, after the commission's report was published, the GULAG administration later overruled 22 of the camp management's decisions.

A medical investigation carried out the day after the action revealed that 34 prisoners had been severely injured by blows to the head, back, face and other parts of the body. The doctor recommended that 22 of the prisoners should for this reason be sent for two weeks to the camp sick-bay.

After several visits to the camp, the KPK's emissary revealed that the supply, handling and distribution of foodstuffs, all of which fell under the responsibility of the Ministry of Forestry, were seriously deficient. He believed that part of the reason for this was that prisoners convicted of counter-revolutionary activities had been made to work in the kitchen, and that the latter took every opportunity to incite unrest. However, he also criticized the management for not having seen to the proper provision of food. He had seen himself how 16 tons of meat from Stalingrad had simply been dumped on a dirty floor, whereupon a group of prisoners set to work tearing it into small pieces, which were likewise chucked on the floor. Without being washed, the meat was then thrown straight into brine tubs or cauldrons.

Neither the doctor nor any representative of the management had ever been to the food store, and the KPK's emissary therefore laid the chief responsibility for the disorder on Silantev and Chernov. He also criticized the fact that the camp shop did not sell *makhorka* (a cheap substitute for tobacco), but only expensive cigarettes, which the prisoners could not afford.

In his report, the KPK's emissary supported the prisoners in their complaints about their treatment at the hands of the guards and soldiers. He found that there had been many cases in which prisoners had been shot without justification, and that the use of violence was especially frequent at the work-place and during the transport of prisoners from the camp. The guards often reacted with extreme anger to small breaches of discipline, such as conversing or lighting a cigarette while on the march. Prisoners were ordered to lie on their stomachs (irrespective of the state of the roads), and if they refused, a salvo was fired over their heads. In the period 1952–53 eight prisoners were shot dead. The envoy from Moscow believed that part of the explanation for the large consumption of cartridges could be that shots were used as a means of communication between the centre and the outposts of the camp. The punishment cells and the strict regime were also used arbitrarily, without explaining to those concerned the reason for the punishment.

One prisoner told the investigating commission that he had been transferred to the camp in 1950. In the two months before the strike he and his fellow prisoners had eaten nothing but sugar and bread, since the rest of the food had been inedible. They had complained on numerous occasions, but nothing had happened. In addition the management had also stinted on wages, while work norms had been increased. He related how on 31 May all the prisoners had decided to go on hunger strike with the aim of attracting Moscow's attention. At the same time he confirmed that the head of the camp had come to the camp on 1 June and reported that fresh food supplies had been brought, that the work norms would be reduced and wages paid. The prisoners however responded by saying that they would continue the strike until they were granted a dialogue with Moscow.[9]

The prisoner described the guards' conduct on 4 June as particularly heavy-handed. He related how 70–80 soldiers had come into the barracks and ordered the prisoners immediately to leave. They were told that if they did not obey they would be thrashed. Without waiting for an answer, the soldiers began to drag the prisoners off their bunks and lay about with handcuffs, belts and truncheons. Other prisoners were sitting on the roofs outside and saw how the prisoners were driven crawling out of the barracks. Many received severe blows to the head. There were over 200 soldiers in the camp. The prisoner had recognized Chernov and other officers, who not only had failed to stop the attacks, but had themselves taken part in them. The prisoners were put in handcuffs and waited for three hours before they were loaded into trains and taken away.

The prisoner went on to report that the guards frequently fired shots after them. During his long period in camp he had seen several people shot when they had attempted to escape – even after they had given themselves up and were standing with their hands in the air. In his view, the guards at this camp behaved worse than the German prison guards had done during the war.

Another prisoner similarly reported that the guards were brutal, that the cabbage was like soap, the meat infested with bugs and the fish rotten. The work norms had been increased so that it was impossible to earn anything, and finally all these things had become too much. He also said that soldiers had entered the barracks and immediately started beating up the prisoners. Outside they had had to run the gauntlet of two lines of soldiers. One of the officers allegedly said: 'You were expecting a commission from Washington, and instead you got Stalingrad!'

Altogether 10 prisoners testified to the KPK, and their testimony was very consistent. They confirmed that the strike represented an organized protest first and foremost against violence and arbitrary behaviour on the part of the guards. They also supported the contention that this had been characteristic of camp conditions all along, and that the barrel of rotten fish had simply been the last straw which had led to all the stored-up discontent and anger among the prisoners finally being unleashed.

The camp commandant, Silantev, was obliged to answer a long list of critical questions from the KPK concerning conditions in the camp and the circumstances surrounding the prisoners' protests. Like his superior from the GULAG, he attempted to pass on the responsibility. He informed the KPK that he and the camp's state prosecutor, Yakolev, had been taken to Section 16 on 1 June and had attempted to get the prisoners to break off the strike. When they failed to do so, he had phoned the head of the GULAG, Dolgikh, and asked him to send a delegation from Moscow. He had emphasized that this had been one of the prisoners' demands, and that in his opinion it could have assured a peaceful end to the strike. As we already know, Dolgikh had turned down this request and asked Silantev to solve the conflict himself.

According to Silantev, Dolgikh's refusal had put him in a difficult situation, since he had promised at a meeting with the prisoners not only to make sure that the food improved, but to meet their demand for a dialogue with Moscow. If Silantev was speaking the truth, it was unjust at least that the entire blame for the outcome of events should have been placed on him alone.

Silantev made a further attempt to justify himself on the grounds that when the strike broke out he had had only a few months' experience as the leader of the camp and had therefore relied on his deputy, Colonel Nosov, an experienced man whom he had not had any reason to distrust. He had therefore left the management of the action itself to Nosov and signed the latter's false reports concerning the uprising. Later, however, Silantev weakened this defence by revealing that when he himself was the deputy in the camp he had already noted irregularities in Nosov's discharge of his duties. He must therefore have turned a blind eye to his subordinate's immoral behaviour and on several occasions demonstrated that he was ignorant of the real conditions in the camp.

Silantev stubbornly insisted that the strike had been instigated by a small group of hardened criminals who had forced the ordinary prisoners to join them. However, he again weakened this argument by his subsequent testimony at the hearing. Asked why they had decided to make all the prisoners leave the barracks, he answered that it was precisely because they had been afraid that the ordinary prisoners would protect 'the bandits' if they attempted to single the latter out in the barracks themselves.

In his concluding statement Silantev requested Shkiryatov, in deciding on his punishment, to bear in mind that since joining the MVD in 1939, and until he was appointed to the camp in 1952, he had been employed only doing office work in Moscow. The uprising had begun only two weeks after he was appointed head of the camp and he had no experience of how these kinds of problems should be solved. He pointed out, moreover, that his appointment as commandant had coincided with an overall restructuring of the whole camp system and the introduction of the widespread amnesty, which was immensely complicated. In May and June alone he had had to deal with 20,000 individual instances of release or reduced sentences. His short period of tenure combined with the heavy workload had made it impossible for him to go out to the various sections of the camp and look into conditions there. Finally, he asked the KPK to bear in mind that the prisoners in Section 16 were the worst elements and trouble-makers in the camp, who had been drawn not just from the central camp but from other camps. They continuously broke the rules and provoked and insulted the guards, and in his opinion this partially accounted for the attack which some of the guards launched on 4 June.[11]

Sergei Nikolaevich Chernov, the head of Section 16, testified to the KPK's envoy that he, Silantev and the camp's state prosecutor, Yakovlev, had visited the prisoners on 1 June and attempted to get them to eat. But they were met only with abuse and demands for a commission from Moscow.[12] Alone among those who gave testimony, Chernov related how on 2 June the authorities had attempted to move 64 prisoners from the strict to the ordinary-regime zone. However, the prisoners had not wanted to leave the barracks and resisted the move – because, according to Chernov, they had been threatened by 'the hard core'. The prisoners, he said, had shouted abuse and curses at the camp managers and guards. There were also threats such as: 'If you so much as approach one of the sections, we will set the barracks alight and reduce the whole zone to ashes. If you come into the barracks, we'll tear you to pieces!' The management felt so threatened that they finally gave up their enterprise and left the area.

The state prosecutor, Yakovlev, informed the investigating commission that it was he who had had the idea of transferring the 64 prisoners to ordinary regime. He had got backing for the plan at a meeting with Silantsev, Nosov and Chernov on 1 June, and had immediately set about preparing the necessary documents. The decision was based on the supposition that the majority of the prisoners in strict regime would be willing to break off the strike and come out of the strict zone. As we know, the plan did not succeed, because the prisoners refused to be moved. In his testimony Yakovlev laid the blame for this on Silantsev, whom he considered 'arrogant'. The latter had scheduled the action for late in the evening, and none of the prisoners would go along with that – partly because of the timing, and partly because they didn't know where they were going. Given the prisoners' strong resistance, this explanation seems unconvincing and appears to be nothing but an attempt on Yakovlev's part to justify himself before the investigating commission. The resistance on 2 May was probably also the reason for the management's nervousness about the action on 4 June.

Like the other managers Chernov claimed that the strike and other forms of unrest in the camp, both on this and on other occasions, had been instigated by a small group of hardened criminals. He told the investigating commission:

> 'The strike was set in motion by a group on whom decent words had no effect, who used the slightest pretext to stir things up, and who dragged in prisoners who would otherwise have submitted to the positive influence of labour.'

The interesting point in Chernov's statement is his admission that ordinary prisoners were to be found among the strikers.

On 30 October 1953 the Ministry of Justice took over the case from the camp management. In the indictment it was said that the authorities had resolved to punish severely those involved in order to counter lawlessness and arbitrary behaviour in the camps. The commandant of the camp, Colonel Silantsev, was dismissed and at the same time deprived of his status as an official of the Ministry of Justice and reduced to doing ordinary work within the GULAG administration. His next in command, Colonel Nosov, who was responsible for discipline among the prisoners, was fired and tried by a military tribunal. Lieutenant General Dolgikh, the head of the GULAG, was told to make sure that conditions were regulated in the camps.[13]

The State Prosecutor of the Soviet Union dealt with the case of the camp's state prosecutor, Yakovlev. In his ruling he pointed out that Yakovlev had failed to intervene to deal with the extremely unsatisfactory conditions in the camp, and that he had therefore been removed from his post. Criticism was levelled at the food and especially at the fact that disciplinary measures had been misused and had not served any educative purpose among the prisoners. Only the harshest methods, in the form of imposing strict-regime condition, had been employed. Instead of meeting the prisoners' just demands, Yakovlev had tacitly seen to it that they were brought out of their barracks and beaten up by the soldiers and guards.[14]

The prisoners' organized protest in the Kargapolskii camp was the culmination of long-endured suppression and injustice. It was clear that it was not just the hard core that had been behind the protest, as the camp management had claimed, but that it had the widespread backing of other prisoners. We have seen how the prisoners, wise from experience, did not trust the local representative of power, and therefore demanded that they deal directly with Moscow. This was indicative of their belief that it was the local authorities who were responsible for the bad conditions, and that the top Party leaders would intervene if they got to hear how bad matters really were. This assumption is familiar from the numerous letters sent by prisoners in the camps to Stalin, and indeed it dates back to tsarist times; but there is little to suggest that it was this tradition which prevailed, in this particular case – or at least their assumption in this instance was not a case of false consciousness, since it was precisely the central authorities, in the form of the KPK, who, as we have seen, ensured the prisoners' victory.

The case testifies to the sluggishness of the executive branch of Soviet power, which exercised a brake on the political leadership's resolution to adjust their policy on prisoners in the camps. The sudden reversal of policy had given rise to a sense of insecurity and confusion among the middle ranks – meaning in this instance the camp management and functionaries, who were inclined to solve problems by applying traditional methods. It is striking in this connection that the leaders who were called to account for their mistakes attempted to exculpate themselves and to push the responsibility onto others, both colleagues and superiors. It is also striking that the state prosecutor should have passed a judgment so straightforward and unequivocal. There was no doubt as to the facts of the matter or as to who was to blame, and the prisoners' demands were recognized as just.

The uprising in Steplag, May–June 1954

The uprising started on 17 May 1954. On the night of 17–18 May a group of 400 male prisoners from Section 3 of the camp had torn down the walls and thronged into the women's section. The guards had tried in vain to stop them by shooting, as a result of which 13 prisoners had been killed. This was the starting point for the most dramatic and long-lasting uprising in a Soviet prison camp that has so far come to light. In response to the shooting, the majority of the approximately 5,000 prisoners in the section refused the following day to go to work until the guards were brought to account for their actions.

What had apparently begun as a spontaneous action developed into an organized protest against the arbitrary nature of camp life and the penal system, leading eventually to an armed assault by the authorities on 26 June. Despite persistent attempts on the part of the authorities to use a combination of persuasion and threats to get the prisoners to give up their enterprise, they continued to extend and fortify the occupied area. A strike committee was established to deal with the authorities, which, besides the camp management itself, consisted of such prominent figures as the head of the GULAG administration and the Deputy Minister of the Interior, who had been sent out from Moscow as soon as it became apparent what was happening in the camp.

Ten days after the occupation by Section 3, a meeting took place between the authorities and the prisoners. It was held in the camp's canteen, where some 2,000 people gathered. The prisoners' spokesman, Kuznetsov, set out a series of demands to the camp management. In the first place they requested an investigation into the events of the night of 17–18 May which had led to the rebellion, and into other cases in which prisoners had been shot during 1954. They asked for guarantees that the prisoners' spokesman would not be prosecuted in the event that the action was called off. Demands were made for prisoners to receive the same wages and working conditions as voluntary workers, for the abolition of the punishment cells and for free communication between the men's and women's sections in the camp. The prisoners wanted a reduction in punishment for those who had been sentenced to 25 years' imprisonment and an abolition of the rule of exile for those prisoners who had already served their sentences. Finally, they requested that a member of the Presidium of the Central Committee should be involved in the negotiations. The prisoners' demands were not narrowly political, but they all had in common a desire for the introduction of more humane conditions in the camp. The very fact that the meeting took place, and that the authorities embarked on negotiations, must have strengthened the prisoners' belief that it was possible for them to do something to change conditions themselves.

Immediately after the meeting the head of the GULAG, I. Dolgikh, issued a decree. It stated that those responsible for the use of weapons against the prisoners on 17–18 May would be fired and charged. With regard to working conditions, the prisoners were promised eight hours' uninterrupted rest, and as far as a reduction in punishment was concerned, long-term prisoners who were mentally ill or suffering an incurable disease, together with those prisoners who had committed their crime before they were 18 years old, were to be released. The latter point was included in a decree from the Ministry of the Interior on 13 May and was therefore not directly related to the actual conflict. As can be seen, no general reduction in the punishment for long-term prisoners was offered, nor any guarantee for the prisoners' spokesman; nothing was said about the possibility of association between the men and women in the camp, nor, finally, about a visit from a member of the Presidium of the Central Committee. In other words, there was only a partial attempt to meet the prisoners' demands, and this was the reason for their continuing the action.

On 5 June the prisoners were given a further indication that the authorities were willing to talk to them. On that day Dolgikh made a speech, which was broadcast over the camp's internal radio.[15] The speech included threats, but also concessions. Thus Dolgikh expressed his willingness to embark on a discussion of questions concerning a general reduction in the sentences of long-term prisoners, the payment of wages and a visit from one of the senior politicians. Following the meeting on 18 May the prisoners put forward a request that sentences be reduced by five days for every day on which they over-fulfilled their work norm. Dolgikh also offered a guarantee that none of the members of the prisoners' strike committee would be charged by the authorities. The condition was, however, that they give up their action 'in time'. One may assume that, in the view of the authorities, the prisoners were already close to breaking this deadline, but Dolgikh did not mention any particular time limit.

In an attempt to bring the prisoners to their senses, and presumably also with the aim of widening the division between the radicals and the more cool-headed prisoners, Dolgikh listed all the improvements that had already been introduced in the camps: the large-scale amnesty for 50 per cent of prisoners, the introduction of ordinary regime for all, wages for work, and the general amnesty for prisoners who were under the age of 18 when they were convicted, together with those who were mentally or incurably ill. Finally, he gave concrete examples of releases of prisoners from Steplag. There is no doubt that, in Dolgikh's view, these improvements were very radical, and that in this context the prisoners may have seemed to him ungrateful. Presumably this attitude also underlay his view that the uprising had been instigated and carried on by a small group of 'bandits' who kept the majority under control through force and violence. In his radio speech they were characterized as follows: 'There are plenty of troublemakers who want to live loosely and to satisfy their lowest instincts; they want to have idleness, parties, racketing and women.'

Undoubtedly there was some disagreement among the prisoners, and they were not 100 per cent behind the uprising. But Dolgikh's view of the circumstances must nevertheless be seen as one-sided and distorted. It is improbable that a small group could have held around 5,000 people under their control for 40 days.

From a report to the Minister of the Interior, Kruglov, dated 15 June, it is evident that the local authorities viewed developments in the occupied section of the camp with growing alarm. The prisoners showed no sign of giving in. On the contrary, they intensified their demands, and continued to extend the barricades and other defenses. Plans were also being laid to manufacture primitive weapons and explosives. The instigators of this plan were allegedly a group of Baltic prisoners who could draw on their experience in the resistance struggle against Soviet power. They also tried, with some success, to make contact with prisoners in other sections of the camp and with ordinary citizens in the nearby town, with the help of radio equipment and leaflets attached to kites, from which they were released and scattered over the areas outside the camp.

On 20 June the Council of Ministers received a letter from two officials from the Ministry of Industry[17] The ministers were extremely dissatisfied with the fact that the Ministry of the Interior had still not fulfilled its promise to re-establish order in the Steplag. This had had a serious impact on production figures in the region's metal industry, which would not be able to fulfil its plans. The ministers pointed out that the situation was further aggravated by the fact that the MVD had not kept to an agreement to bring 4,000 more convict workers into the area in March and April. Only 1,400 had been brought in, of whom the majority had refused to work.

The letter ended with a request that normal conditions be restored within 10 days. Within six days the authorities forcibly intervened. This was not because of the letter from the Ministry alone; but there is good reason to believe that the economic argument played a central role. In all the authorities' appeals to the prisoners in the camp the demand for a return to work was given highest priority. This testifies to the fact that to a greater degree than previously the camps had become economic entities, and that the most important criterion of success for both the camp management and the Ministry of the Interior was the maintenance of stable production.

Further evidence to support this view was given in an instruction sent by the Ministry of the Interior to Yegorov on 24 June detailing what measures should be taken in order to launch an assault on the occupied camp.[18] In addition to five T-34 tanks, fire engines, dogs and soldiers should be brought in. It was stressed that the aim of the action was to isolate and neutralize the 'criminal elements' and deprive them of their influence over those prisoners who no longer wanted to be part of the action. The camp management was told under all circumstances to avoid causing deaths. For this reason experienced officers should be used who would ensure that weapons would be employed only against those prisoners who directly attacked the soldiers and guards.

The armed assault on Section 3 of the camp was set in motion early in the morning of 26 June. According to a report to the Ministry of the Interior, the prisoners had been warned in advance over the radio and urged not to resist. At the same time, however, it was claimed that the assault came as a surprise, and that the resistance had therefore not been as violent as had been feared.[19]

The biggest problems arose with those prisoners who had barricaded themselves into six of the camp barracks, and with a group of 500 men and women who had gathered in the main entrance of the women's section. According to the report, the prisoners were armed with home-made hand grenades, pistols, lances, iron bars, clubs and stones. The tanks deployed fired only blanks, while the soldiers and guards used rockets loaded with live cartridges, pistols and rifles. According to documents of the Ministry of Interior, 35 prisoners were killed, while there were no losses on the side of the assailants.

The authorities tried persistently to present the uprising as a violent attempt on the part of a small group of prisoners to force their fellow prisoners into committing crimes against the Soviet state in the form of strikes and other kinds of insubordination. There is no doubt that the core of the uprising originated with a relatively limited group, but it is difficult to imagine how the prisoners in the barricaded camp would have been able to withstand 40 days under severe pressure from the authorities had it not gained widespread backing. The sources do not tell us anything about the more fundamental reasons for the up-rising. One may assume, however, that the prisoners were influenced in their action by the atmosphere of the times, which had given them faith that through action and negotiation they could obtain concrete improvements in their conditions. This belief was probably strength-ened by the fact that the authorities did indeed enter rapidly into negotiations, in the course of which they made a number of concrete concessions and held out the prospect of others.

9
Mass Unrest

In this section we will investigate three examples of mass unrest, which took place in three different years during the rule of Khrushchev: in Kemerovo in 1955, Karaganda in 1959 and Novocherkassk in 1962.

Kemerovo, 1955

In September 1955 an overwhelming majority of the 3,233 conscripts at a building project in Kemerovo, 'Trust 96,' refused to go to work.[1] The conscripts in question were young men who in 1952 had been called up to do their army service in a construction battalion. In 1954 they were prematurely moved to the reserves, but at the same time informed that they should remain at their station until their term of conscription expired on 1 October 1955. In the meantime, however, a decree was issued by the Ministry that this date should be put back to 1 April 1956. When word of this reached the soldiers, they refused to work. According to the report on the incident, the situation had already been tense even before the decree was issued because of the miserable conditions in which the conscripts lived and worked.

On 10 September 1955 a group of several hundred workers in the construction battalion invaded the headquarters of 'Trust 96'. Furniture and offices were smashed up and the director of the enterprise, Stepanenko, was captured and led away. He must subsequently have escaped, for on 12 September the conscripts once again stormed his offices and tried to force him to discharge them. The following day, having failed to get their way, over 1,000 workers occupied several public buildings, including the local military headquarters. They also succeeded in getting into the headquarters of 'Trust 96' where the offices were again ransacked and the deputy director, Kofman, together with the head of personnel, was forcibly captured and led away. Prior to this some of the conscripts had attempted to push Kofman out of a window on the third floor.

On the same day the strikers burst into a mass meeting organized by the Party in the city stadium. We can only guess at the purpose of the meeting, but doubtless it was intended to damp down local anger. Instead, the leader of the strike took over the meeting, gave a thrashing to the organizers, captured the director of 'Trust 96' and marched him back to the headquarters of the enterprise, accompanied by a thousand-strong band of workers. Here the strikers finally succeeded in forcing him to give them a discharge.[2]

From the authorities' analysis of the cause of the unrest it is clear that they were aware that working conditions and housing problems had played an important role. The workers had constantly been moved from one project to another, and there had been long periods where they had nothing to do. The fault lay in poor organization and lack of supplies. Moreover, there were problems with wages and work discipline. For one reason or another, somewhere between 10 and 20 per cent of the work-force were absent on any given day. As far as housing was concerned, it was alleged that the roofs were leaky and the plaster falling from the ceilings. There were no cooking facilities, and, as the report put it, the food in the canteens left much to be desired. On top of all this, neither the Party nor the Komsomol had undertaken any kind of political or educational work among the conscripts.[3]

The main reason for the unrest had been the announcement that the conscripts' period of service was to be extended. The blame for this was laid on the local commander. He should have ensured that the workers were prepared for the extension and that they understood that this was a central rather than a local decision. It would appear that the local commander had been used as a scapegoat. Even had he had the backing of an active propaganda apparatus, it seems unlikely that he could have succeeded in persuading the soldiers to remain at their posts longer than was absolutely necessary.

In their analysis, the authorities maintain that a significant propor-tion of the workers joined in the action. Nevertheless, they had felt called upon to identify a core of instigators who could be brought to court. Thus five individuals were subsequently tried and sentenced to up to seven years in prison and labour camp, with confiscation of property and denial of voting rights.

The events in Kemerovo in September 1955 were described in official language as mass disturbances. The description seems apt, since the vast majority of the approximately 3,000 demobilized soldiers took part in one way or another. By all accounts the action became at times quite violent. The offices at the headquarters were destroyed, and several members of the management were subjected to threats and physical violence. Altogether, then, this was a serious case, and in this context the sentences meted out to the 'instigators' seem surprisingly mild. One explanation may be that, compared with the subsequent uprising in Novocherkassk, the unrest in Kemerovo was, despite everything, a local affair, and it therefore seemed less crucial to the authorities to make an example of it.

Karaganda, 1959

Following the 21st Party Congress at the beginning of 1959, when the economic and political triumphs of recent years, not least the Soviet space programme, had been celebrated, and the Party had bubbled over with optimism; and following his invitation, in June that year, to visit the USA, Khrushchev ran into an uncomfortable and serious problem. For a time it seems to have brought him down from the heights of enthusiasm to the reality of Soviet life, which, as he admitted to those closest to him, was not anywhere near so promising.

On 3 August he learned, through a telephone call from the First Secretary of the Communist Party in Kazakhstan, N.J. Belyaev, that at a gigantic building project in the city of Temirtau near Karaganda, where for the last ten years the construction of a steel plant had been in progress, there had been violent clashes between groups of young workers and the authorities. It subsequently emerged that 11 workers had been killed and several hundred wounded. The situation was all the more uncomfortable for the political leadership because this was a so-called 'Komsomol project' in which most of the workers – some 25,000 in all – were recruited from the generation that was supposed to be building communism within the next 20 years.[4]

In 1939 there had been 5,000 inhabitants of Temirtau, where the steel works were being constructed. By 1959 the figure had reached 54,000, of which roughly half were employed at the construction site. Despite the fact that the work had been going on for a decade, the workers lived in such primitive accommodation as tents, railways carriages and barracks with no running water or toilets. Drinking water had to be fetched from a long way away, and was seldom sufficient. These living conditions were all the more burdensome because the summers were very warm and the winters cold.

The miserable housing and the poor state of supplies, which were typical of the huge building projects of the 1930s, led in 1959, as they had done earlier, to a big turnover in the workforce and to irritation and quarrelling among those who stayed. Alcoholism, gambling and fighting were rife. The Party's educational work was confined to distributing the Party newspaper. There were no cultural institutions to provide diversion for the workers during their free time.

The work itself also left much to be desired. Not a day went by without some work stoppage, technical breakdown or industrial accident. Progress was constantly impeded by the failure of suppliers to honour agreements for the delivery of building materials and equipment.

Leaders at both regional and republican level were well aware of the state of affairs at the construction site, but this did not prevent them, at conferences and on other occasions, from presenting the situation in positive and optimistic terms. It is surprising, indeed, that the social explosion did not occur until 1959; but this can perhaps be explained by the fact that many of the workers left after a short time, so that the turnover was very high.

When the workers from the first shift left the construction site on the evening of 1 August 1959, they could not find a single canteen open. This aroused great indignation, and was probably the spark which set fire to the blaze the following day. On Sunday, large groups consisting mainly of young workers went on the rampage in the shops, stores and canteens. Once all the goods had been seized, everything else was smashed up. There were also incidents of arson and attacks on public buildings.

By the evening, normal life in the town and at the building site had come to a halt. Workers had downed tools, and the unrest continued. The authorities intervened by sending in militia and guards from a nearby prison camp. Despite using weapons, they were unable to put a stop to the disturbances, and on Monday regular troops were therefore sent in. Five thousand men, led by General Zapevalin, arrived from the prison camp. The soldiers were flown in from, among other places, Novosibirsk, Omsk and Barnaul. The actual figures have not been revealed, but the number of cities involved indicates that it was a very significant number.

Judging from documents of the state prosecution, 16 people lost their lives in the clashes. Eleven were killed during the struggle, while five died later of their injuries. The army revealed that none of the soldiers had died, but 11 were wounded by bullets.

The local Party authorities were not very keen to get involved or to take responsibility for solving the crisis. It seems that at first this was no more than an ordinary disturbance, of a kind which was apparently quite routine, and which could be resolved without their intervention. When it emerged that the situation was critical, they timidly held back. Thus the leader of the *obkom* refused to meet the workers, and was said to have given the following good advice to one of the military leaders: 'Keep away, they'll do away with you.'[5]

The first secretary of the Communist Party of Kazakhstan, Belyaev, was in Moscow at the beginning of August. When he realized the gravity of the situation, he gave orders by telephone that a group of loyal Communists should be established locally to make personal contact with the troublemakers. Less than two hours later over 2,000 Party members were summoned for a meeting, but for fear of what might befall them, the local leaders refused to put the plan into practice. They were not totally paralysed, however. On the first evening of the disturbances they made sure that two of the trouble-makers were arrested. However, the latter were released the very next morning under pressure from several thousand demonstrators.

It took over two months to normalize the situation in the town. The authorities used two means to bring this about: military control and a rapid and noticeable improvement in working and living conditions. With regard to the latter, fresh foods of a kind that had never been seen before quickly turned up in the canteens and shops. Radios were installed in the barracks and televisions were found. A hospital with 400 beds was rapidly built.

Following the disturbances there was a court case in which the leaders of the local Party and soviet were charged with responsibility for what had happened. As a result, the First Secretary of the *obkom* and the director of the construction project were removed from their posts and later expelled from the Party. But few if any could seriously have believed that the problem was thereby solved. The authorities were well aware of the real core of the problem: namely, that production always took priority over people's needs. Already in the 1930s Ordzonikidze, who had then been in charge of heavy industry, had recognized this problem. He said: 'We always talk in the first instance of factories, metal and coal, and only afterwards of human beings; it should be the other way round.'[6]

As already discussed, Khrushchev's reforms were intended to do away with this Soviet tradition, but the events in Karaganda – and undoubtedly in many other places – were an uncomfortable reminder that, even in the late fifties, circumstances worked against establishing this essential condition for the positive development of the economy and life in general. In a conversation with his son-in-law Adzubei, Khrushchev is claimed to have said:

> 'We began the year so well, we set great goals, we wanted to over-take America, but in reality we've disgraced ourselves, we're acting just as we used to do; we haven't changed our methods of manage-ment; we aim to solve everything through force, instead of thinking in terms of people, and then we end up shooting young boys. It's not just a case of the building project in Kazakhstan – it's not neces-sarily better elsewhere. We have to change our methods and boldly bring our young people to the fore, but here they've been treated in the old timers' way. The accident in Karaganda is a danger signal; that's not the way to build communism; we won't overtake America by going back to Stalin.'[7]

What Khrushchev did not want, or rather, perhaps, was unable to see was that the solution to the problem depended not on people so much as on the economic system, where, fundamentally, it was still the figures for gross production that counted. It was the quantity of blast furnaces and not the welfare of workers that could forward a Party leader's career.

Novocherkassk, 1962

On 17 May 1962, at a meeting of the Central Committee of the Communist Party, approval was given to a proposal from the Council of Ministers to raise the state purchase and sale price of meat products.[8] The agreement introduced average price rises of around 30 per cent with effect from 1 June. From a strictly economic point of view the action was well justified, since the agricultural sector was in a wretched condition and a critical shortage of food products had arisen in the shops. The problem was however linked to the artificial lowering of food prices instituted by Stalin after the war. This move had reduced the peasants' already extremely poor living conditions, while on the other hand significantly contributing to the regime's popularity among city people. The sources indicate that especially among the latter the price rises of 1962 were met with bewilderment, insecurity and anger, while in rural areas there was a tendency to see them as part of the government's endeavour to relieve the situation for the peasants. For the urban population in particular the initiative thus presented a glaring contrast not only to Stalin's 'generosity', but also to Khrushchev's foolhardy claims that the building of communism was already in progress and should be completed by 1980, and that the Soviet Union would soon overtake the USA with regard to the individual citizen's consumption of food. Although the government and the Party attempted openly and seriously to explain the need for the price rises, it was inevitable that this action would give rise to profound social unrest. It contributed significantly to deepening the divide between the population's immediate experience and the Party's propaganda, and thus to strengthening discontent with both the First Secretary of the Party and the regime.

The situation had arisen as a consequence of the mistaken agricultural policy which had been pursued especially since 1957. By 1960, declaring that its aim was to overtake the USA in the consumption of meat and milk, the Party had already launched an attack on the last remnants of private activity in the agricultural sector. Private agriculture was regarded not only as being unproductive and uneconomic but also as an ideologically undesirable relic from the past. Now the final push towards collectivization must be carried out. Private plots were reduced, and the right to keep privately owned animals was curtailed. At the same time further pressure was put on the *sovkhozes* and *kolkhozes* to produce more grain, meat and milk. The policy was to prove counter-productive. Collective production would not immediately make up for the decline in the private sector. In 1960 rationing had to be introduced, and the consumption of agricultural produce fell markedly.

In reports to the Central Committee on public opinion, assurances were made that an overwhelming majority of the population had understood the government's policy in the 'correct light'. However, mention was also made of the fact that the policy had given rise to discontent and criticism and in particular cases to open resistance. The reports from the Party's departments were generally more optimistic than the KGB's. But between 1 and 4 June signs of growing concern about the extent and nature of the resistance can be detected in both organizations.

One type of positive reaction may be summarized in the statement: 'If the government has taken this action it must be because it was necessary'. Statements of this type bear witness to a passive identity, which led to the individual's simply accepting the regime's decisions and adapting him or herself accordingly. Another type of acceptance, closely related to the first, might be summed up as willingness to accept anything so long as a new war could be avoided. A third type might be designated 'conditional acceptance', whereby the government's action was approved in so far as it was expected to improve living standards. This form of acceptance left room for possible conflict if the government's policy failed to yield the promised and expected results. A fourth type of acceptance might be described as critical. The price rises were regarded as a step towards correcting those mistakes that had previously been perpetrated against the peasants. Thus, for example, it was said: 'While we were laying the foundations of industry, we neglected agriculture. We should long ago have done something in this area; had we done so, we could have avoided this explosive price rise.'[9] A fifth type of acceptance came from members of the peasantry, who saw the government's action as a significant step towards normalizing rural conditions. Obeisance such as the following was thus made to the Party: 'Thanks to our dear Party, our government and to N.S. Khrushchev personally for their concern ... '.[10]

It seems that resistance to the price rises developed most dramatically in Novocherkassk in the Rostov region, where it led to direct confrontations between the population and the authorities. The events were mentioned and analysed in the reports from the KGB and local Party departments to the Central Committee and Khrushchev. It appears from these that the immediate cause of the strikes and demonstrations, in which between five and ten thousand people took part, was the government's price policy. The KGB's assurances to Khrushchev, that all possible forces had been moved in to prevent the spreading of rumours and other information from Novocherkassk, suggest that they were nervous lest these dramatic events should spread to other parts of the country. Judging from the reports, the atmosphere was indeed very tense in many places. Tighter censorship of mail and surveillance of traffic to and from the region were introduced. Moreover, from the first days of the conflict high-ranking members of the political leadership were brought into the city. Before going into the history of these events, we will first look in more detail at the more sporadic protests which, according to the reports, were taking place elsewhere.

Calls for strikes were reported in the cities of Ivanovo, Magnitogorsk, Tambov, Donetsk and Leningrad. In a great many cities leaflets were handed out and slogans written on pavements, walls and hoardings. There were many coarse and insulting attacks on named political leaders. Khrushchev, whose popularity had steeply declined during the previous few years, frequently came under fire. There were also oral calls for protest in the form of strikes, demonstrations and even violent revolt. Finally, examples of resistance from private conversations and letters were also reported.

The leader of the KGB, Semichastnyi, reported to the Central Committee in the summer of 1962 that he had registered a significant rise in anti-Soviet activity throughout the country in connection with the price rises. Around 7,000 anti-Soviet leaflets and pamphlets were confiscated. This was 100 per cent more than in the same period the previous year. These communications contained attacks on the leaders of the Communist Party and nationalistic declarations, and demonstrated a lack of faith in communism in the Soviet Union. Hostility was stirred up towards individual leaders of the Party and towards the Party itself, and there were threats directed at local leaders. Around 1,000 instigators were arrested, among them 364 workers (34 per cent), 192 functionaries, 210 students, 108 unemployed, 105 pensioners and 60 *kolkhoz* members.[11] It is noteworthy that more than half came from the most poorly educated section of the population.

Their criticisms can be divided into several different types that reflected different degrees of insight and various ideological and political attitudes. To the first type belong those criticisms that resulted from the experience of a growing disparity between ideology and reality. This experience was not confined to this period alone, but had been exacerbated by the fact that after Stalin's death, and especially after the 20th Party Congress, there had been great expectations of changes and improvements in the near future. Khrushchev's assurances of constantly growing welfare for all had contributed to this atmosphere. When it became apparent that all of this amounted to little more than words, discontent grew and the propaganda became increasingly counter-productive. A worker from Riga was reported to have made the following observation in a conversation with colleagues: 'In the newspapers they write that the people have approved the Party's and the government's decision. But that's not so. There are many that don't approve it.'[12] A doctor was reported to have said that the price rises were yet further evidence that communism would never become a reality, and that it was all a question of empty words.[13] An electrician from the Novgorod region pointed out that there was a gap between the policy pursued and the promises made at the 22nd Party Congress.[14] A female worker at a factory in Perm expressed her view briefly and precisely as follows: 'Nowhere do they tell you the truth. There is no one in the leadership that one can believe.'[15]

The growing schism between words and practice created a particular problem for the Party's agitators. Thus a worker from Moscow was puzzled at hearing a Party emissary claim at a meeting about the international situation that the rumours of price rises in the Soviet Union were just hostile propaganda from BBC radio, when it was obvious that the radio station was correct.[16]

A number of Party agitators apparently found themselves in difficulties over government and Party policy. A teacher from Belilovskaya said: 'In my discussions with people I have always relied on our magnificent programme. I spoke about the uninterrupted material growth for the workers. What am I to say now? They simply won't believe any longer what I say.'[17] Lieutenant Kovalchuk from the Black Sea fleet declared: 'I don't support the Communist Party's move and will not therefore agitate on this matter among the soldiers.'[18] Captain Andianov from the Engineers Corps reportedly said: 'With what weapon will our ideology now struggle against capitalist ideology? It is becoming difficult to work with the soldiers.'[19]

The reports provide both direct and indirect evidence that the Party's promises concerning improvements in the material situation played a central role in legitimizing the regime. The direct criticism of the price rises and the agitators' concern about them testify to this. A well-known actor, who apparently often visited the West, was quoted as making the following criticism of Soviet propaganda: 'If only they would shut up about our already overtaking America. It is disgusting to have to listen to loudspeakers all day long saying we, we, we … . It is just endless and intolerable bragging.'[20]

We have already seen an example of the way in which the BBC played a consciousness-raising role. The sources provide other instances of this. A non-Party worker, Potekhin, from Pyatigorsk, said at a meeting:

> 'In a radio broadcast from England I heard that 70 per cent of national income in the USA goes to the population. There the population lives on the highest level, while here we live on the lowest. All we do is shout about how everything's good here at home, better than everywhere else.'[21]

Engineer Gurov in Penza declared: 'In America there are two million people going hungry; here there are almost 200 million. We feed all our friends, but we're incapable of feeding ourselves.'[22] And there is a further example of a person who was not just discontent with the price rises, but with the Party's programme of support for the other socialist regimes: 'Our government hands out gifts right, left and centre and feeds others, and now we ourselves have nothing to eat. And now they want to get out of this situation at the cost of the workers.'[23]

Initially the protests were few and relatively moderate, but they grew both in radicalism and quantity. In Moscow and other cities slogans against the price rises began appearing here and there on the pavements. Some were more general in character. One example was the doom-laden 'Today – price rises, but what awaits us tomorrow?'[24] In Donetsk the following notice was found, which apart from containing a criticism of those in power called for a struggle: 'They have cheated us, and they are cheating us now. We will fight for justice.'[25] The poster's perception of society as divided into 'us' and 'them' was a typical expression of the population's estrangement from the Party and those in power. A blacksmith from Minsk said: 'We should beat up the communists, they have taken things so far that now they have to raise the price of food.'[26]

The reports include a number of examples of written and oral calls for strikes and demonstrations. A worker in the Vnukovo airport in Moscow said: 'We should meet on Red Square and demand an end to the price rises.'[27] Brigade-leader Romanova said at a meeting at a factory in Moscow: 'The state is fleecing the people. Not only are they raising the price of consumer goods, but the price of food is going up and up. I am sure that there will be strikes at the big plants in Leningrad and Moscow.'[28] A machinist at the Nizhnyi Tagil station is alleged to have declared at a gathering of colleagues: 'Living standards are getting lower and lower, they're reducing wages and raising prices. We can't expect anything good from the present government. We must go on strike and demand an improvement in the standard of living.'[29] The report states that the machinist was sharply repudiated by a majority of the workers gathered. The same happened, according to the material, on other occasions, but in yet other cases the authorities had to intervene. One instance of this can be found in a report on a dock strike in Odessa: 'The leader of the KGB in the Odessa region has received information that several dockworkers at the Ilchevskii docks are intending to refuse to unload foreign ships. The necessary steps have been taken.'[30]

It is evident that the West also played a role in connection with the deliberations over strikes. Two workers in Magnitogorsk were thus reported to have held a conversation in which the following remarks were made: ' ... if the workers would just follow the example of the West and go on strike, the price rises would be repealed straight away.'[31] One worker at a metalworks was quoted as follows: 'We have no democracy in the USSR. So the government makes all sorts of decisions, some of them even damaging to the workers. If the workers weren't so dumb and organized strikes at the factories, as workers in the West do, the government would have to reckon with the working class.'[32]

Against the background of Soviet tradition, demonstrated a few days previously in the regime's armed offensive against the striking workers in Novocherkassk, it could be said that there was very good reason for the workers not simply to import the strike weapon from the West. The statement that everything depended just on the will of the workers crops up again, however, in other reports, and can be interpreted as the outcome of a belief that new times were on the way. The authorities did their utmost to suppress information about the events in Novocherkassk, and it is thus quite probable that nothing was known about them.

It is evident from the material that there were also calls for more radical forms of protest. Timofeev, a worker from a large metalworks in the Chittinsk region, is alleged to have said, at a meeting at the factory where the Central Committee's and Council of Minister's reasons for the price rises were being discussed: 'We should get a machine gun and shoot the lot of them down.'[33] A woman worker in Khabarovsk was reported to have made the following statement: 'Why don't you communists say anything? Power belongs to the people, let us make a revolution.'[34]

Elsewhere too there were calls for revolt. At a meeting at the Kirov factory in Dnepropetrovsk, following an agitation meeting at which a vain attempt had apparently been made to justify the government's policy, the carpenter Taranov went to the deputy head of the department and said: 'We've had enough, the whole lot should be shot down one by one, starting with you and moving upwards.' A soldier was alleged to have said at a military meeting: 'If the people start an uprising now, we're not going to fight against our own people.'[35]

The evidence shows that the price rises in certain cases contributed to promoting a general awareness and to a resulting critique that touched the very core of the system. A woman supervisor at a railway station was reported to have made the following criticism of Khrushchev's restrictions on the peasants' independent activities, which to a considerable extent had helped to provide the population with food:

'It was not right to forbid people in the settlements and villages to keep cattle. If they had let the workers and peasants keep cattle and breed them, this wouldn't have happened, and there would have been enough meat to go round.'[36]

Chief engineer Mestechkin was reported to have made the following statement:

'We heap all the blame for what's bad on Stalin and say that his policies destroyed agriculture. But was it really impossible to revive agriculture after his death? No, there are deeper roots to the decline of agriculture, but apparently we're not allowed to speak about that.'[37]

Both statements reveal an awareness that there existed another way of organizing the economy than the prevailing one. Both present an indirect attack on collectivization and by implication call to reintroduce and strengthen individual activity in agriculture. The reference, discussed earlier, to the exemplary way in which national income was shared in America can also be seen as a radical critique of the Soviet economic system. The calls for strikes, too, can be interpreted as crossing the boundary into a fundamental criticism of the current system: the right to organize and to strike would presuppose the introduction of democratic rights in general.

A particular form of resistance came from those who did not directly attack the system, but who dared to propose alternative solutions to the problem of prices. These proposals were deemed 'petty bourgeois', and in some cases also anti-Soviet, by both the KGB and the Party. As we shall see, both accusations were groundless. The real butt of condemnation was the fact that, instead of merely submitting to the Party's policies, these people had shown individual initiative from below. Their proposals included, for example, keeping the old prices and taxing the highest earners instead; reducing support to the less-developed socialist countries or instead raising the prices of luxury goods such as cars, TVs, refrigerators, vodka and tobacco. A driver from Arkhangelsk reacted with the following totally disillusioned statement: 'Life here gets worse and worse the whole time. Kennedy would be doing the right thing if he dropped an A-bomb over the Soviet Union.[38]

For good reasons, perhaps, humour was in short supply, but the following two statements, which the KGB characterized as anti-Soviet, would have raised a smile elsewhere: 'Eat sawdust soup with a sprinkling of coal!' and 'Eat grass, meat is unnecessary.'[39]

Events at Novocherkassk

'On 2 June 1962 I heard that the radio was announcing a direct broadcast from a concert in the park in my city, Novocherkassk. I looked out of the window and was greatly astonished. I lived right opposite the park, and there wasn't a living soul there. All that could be seen on the streets were armoured cars and patrolling soldiers.'

This account comes from the engineer Gennadii Machevskii. He went on to relate how, after this experience, he sought out his neighbours to discuss the matter with them. This later cost him a great many problems with the authorities, who accused him of having spread 'slanderous rumours.'[40]

The live broadcast of the concert, which never in fact took place, was one of the many efforts the authorities made to cover up the dramatic events in Novocherkassk which occurred between 1 and 3 June 1962. The authorities were nervous lest unrest among the workers at the city's factories should spread to other parts of the country. The background to the unrest was that the economy, after a brief period of bloom, had again begun to show signs of crisis. Delivery of foodstuffs was grinding to a halt, and in many places there were long queues for meat, milk, butter and sometimes even bread. The worse the situation became, the more strident was the Party's propaganda about rapid results and the approaching transition to Communism. Thus as early as October 1961 it had been promised that in the following year the population would reap the benefits of the improved economic policy adopted at the 22nd Party Congress. Instead, as we have seen, the population was given the news on 1 June 1962 that there would be steep price rises in a whole range of food products.

The situation in Novocherkassk was already tense. Not enough housing had been built, so many of the city's workers were sent to live in primitive barracks, where they nevertheless paid high rents. The supply of goods was poor, and, together with a series of major industrial accidents, this had already led to several cases of spontaneous work-stoppages. In addition, at the largest plant in the city – a motor factory – a wage adjustment had been introduced at New Year 1962. For some employees this amounted to a reduction in wages of up to 30 per cent. The news of the price rises on 1 June was the straw that broke the camel's back; and it was at the motor factory that the unrest began.

For the local Party leadership the vital priority was to cover up the events and get the workers to resume work as quickly as possible. Top members of the local Party knew very well that the consequences for themselves could be uncomfortable if Moscow became aware of the problem. However, events quickly took such a turn that they decided nevertheless to involve the central authorities. Moscow reacted immediately. Military units stationed near Novocherkassk were contacted, and high-ranking members of the Party and KGB were immediately sent to the city. All this shows that Moscow took the matter very seriously indeed, which in turn can be interpreted as testimony that the situation was extremely tense not just in Novocherkassk but throughout the country.

Below, we will examine first how the events were reflected in a series of reports from the KGB to the Central Committee and to Khrushchev, including how the central Party authorities, in co-operation with local forces, military units and the Supreme Court suppressed the revolt and dealt with the individuals believed to have instigated the events. The KGB's version of the matter will be set against a series of eyewitness reports which first emerged after *glasnost* and which come from some of the workers involved, as well as other residents of the city.

As discussed earlier, both during the uprising itself and in its aftermath the authorities were at great pains to cover up the events. The local press contains not a single reference to the events before, during or after the uprising.[41] Nor was anything written about them in the central press. On 6 June, to be sure, *Pravda* ran an article about the motor factory in Novocherkassk, but it was devoted exclusively to the workers' unanimous support for the price rises that had been put into effect.

There is also evidence that important archive material subsequently disappeared under more-or-less mysterious circumstances. The journalist Volkov, who on 24 April 1991 published a series of interesting photographs of the events in Novocherkassk, which had reportedly been taken by KGB agents and which were used as evidence in the show trial that followed, relates that he received a photocopy of them from the military prosecutor Aleksandr Tretetskii. Tretetskii himself revealed that he had taken these copies before delivering the originals, together with eight files of archive material relating to the case, to the Soviet Union's State Prosecutor. Subsequently the pictures disappeared.[42]

Two journalists approached the authorities in Rostov in 1989 but were told that they did not possess any documents concerning the case. The officer on duty, A.N. Konovalov, said that out of personal interest he had searched for documents himself, but had not found anything. Nor did an enquiry to the KGB yield any results.[43] Other journalists have revealed that in the late 1980s witnesses of the uprising in Novocherkassk were reluctant to speak to the press. In 1962 the city's residents were informed by the authorities that there had not been any strikes, nor had any shots been fired, or anyone been killed. A woman whose 15-year-old son was shot by soldiers on 2 June was given the same message when she applied at the police station to recover the body.[44] Military personnel were forced under threat to keep their mouths shut after signing the following declaration:

'I, the undersigned, a military officer in the Kamenskii department, commit myself to carrying out the government's instructions and to keeping these a state secret. If I break this promise, I will be subject to the highest penalty, execution. 16.30 hours, 4 June 1962.'[45]

The course of events

After the government's decision on price rises was published on 1 June, 10 foundry workers in the city's largest plant, the motor factory, laid down tools and began discussing the consequences. More workers joined in, and soon around fifty had gathered in the foundry. Representatives from the factory's own Party section tried to get a chance to speak and explain the situation, but were turned down. The same went for the leader of the foundry section, Chernyshkov, who vainly attempted to persuade the workers to resume work. The strikers, who now numbered around 100, went out into the square in front of the factory building, where they engaged the factory director, Kurochkin, in discussion. The situation was tense. The workers demanded an answer from the director as to when safety conditions at the factory would be properly instituted (shortly before, 200 men in one of the factory's departments had been poisoned), and when wages would be settled, and finally protested about the price rises. According to the KGB's report, the director disappeared without making the slightest attempt to pacify the crowd.[46] Witnesses have since given an account of this (evidently decisive) meeting with the workers which puts the director in a more damning light. N. Artemov relates: 'We met with the director, Kurochkin, and asked him what on earth we were going to do. He gave the following impertinent reply: "It isn't that bad, you can just eat pies with offal!"'[47] Artemov regards the director's behaviour as typical of the Stalinist mode of treating workers, but these workers were no longer prepared to put up with this kind of thing. A renewed sense of self-confidence was detectable among them. Another witness claims that one worker, after hearing the director's insulting answer, struck him on the head, whereupon he fled to the administration building.[48]

During the meeting with the director the group of strikers grew to 500. They began to move off and head towards the headquarters of the plant. On the way the strikers began shouting the slogan: 'Meat, milk and higher wages!' The secretaries of both the city's and the factory's Party sections arrived on the scene, and together with KGB officials vainly attempted to persuade the workers to stop the strike. Meanwhile the assembled workers came to a halt in the square in front of the building where the factory management and the leaders of the local Party and the KGB were gathered. The workers demanded that the latter come out and explain themselves, but nothing happened.

Meanwhile a group of workers had stopped the passenger train on the nearby railway and activated the alarm. This resulted in more people pouring in, not just from the factory but also from nearby villages. The crowd in front of the factory headquarters had now reached 5,000. Individual Party members tried to get the chance to speak, but were pushed aside. Some of the workers set about removing the portraits of Party leaders hanging from the facade of the building. Around 4 p.m., when none of the management had yet appeared, a group of workers forced their way into the building and demanded that the managers come out and talk to the crowd. A microphone and loudspeakers were set up on the balcony of the building, and the First Secretary of the Regional Party Committee, Basov, addressed the crowd. He began by reading aloud from the Party's already published explanation of the price rises, but was quickly interrupted by boos and shouts such as 'We can read ourselves!' When the director of the plant, Kurochkin, attempted to speak a shower of stones, bottles and metal objects met him. Several workers thereupon attempted to get hold of the microphone, but the wires to the loudspeakers had been cut. A new group of workers forced their way into the building, allegedly in order to capture of some of the management. The report reveals that a number of KGB agents had infiltrated the crowd of striking workers and were secretly photographing the most active among them. These photos were later used as evidence.

Between 6 and 7 p.m. 220 militiamen were brought in, but were turned away. According to the report, three of them were beaten up. At 8 p.m. five cars and two amoured vehicles with soldiers arrived. They were met with roadblocks and were likewise turned away. The officers were said to have seemed indecisive and paralysed. After one worker had climbed unhindered onto one of the armoured vehicles and attempted to persuade the soldiers to change sides, the vehicles drove away. The meeting continued, and two further attempts to bring soldiers into the area of the factory were prevented.

Meanwhile a group from the train factory had attempted to get the workers from the nearby electrode factory to join in the strike, but was rejected. The communist Vyunenko reportedly threatened to blow up the whole factory if the strikers did not leave.

The following morning, on 2 June, a procession of demonstrators, consisting of workers and their wives and children, marched towards the centre of Novocherkassk. At the head of the demonstration red flags and a portrait of Lenin could be seen. With the help of soldiers, cars and tanks the authorities attempted without opening fire to stop the demonstrators on the bridge over the river Guzlov. However, the demonstration continued towards the headquarters of the city Communist Party, the *gorkom*. On reaching their destination some of the demonstrators began throwing stones at the building, while others forced their way in, tore portraits off the wall, smashed the furniture and beat up Party members and other representatives of power who attempted to stop them.

A number of speeches were made from the building of the *gorkom*, again calling on the soldiers and officers to join the strikers. However, there were no loudspeakers, and the building was surrounded and occupied. According to the KGB documents the demonstrators, who attempted to disarm them, attacked the soldiers and they were therefore forced to open fire. The result was 20 dead – 18 men and two women – and 40 wounded, of whom three later died. The dead were gathered up and secretly buried in various places in the area.

The writer Stanislav Podolskii's description of the events in and around the *gorkom* differs in several critical respects from the KGB's. He claims, to begin with, that the *gorkom* building had already been evacuated when the demonstrators reached it, and that consequently there could not initially have been any confrontation between Party representatives and the demonstrators who went into the building. Podoloskii also claims that individual demonstrators made speeches from the balcony of the building, but unlike the KGB, which stressed the aggressive nature of the demonstrators and represented those involved as violent bandits, he depicts them as peaceful, dignified and self-confident:

> 'I saw around me living, elated faces such as one does not see at "organized demonstrations". There was indignation, irony, impetuousness, scorn and mockery and no sign of indifference or fear. Certain young women in working clothes encouraged the men to stay and obtain justice. There was no question of atrocities or rioting.'[49]

Podolskii relates that one of the demonstrators read aloud a document that he had found in one of the offices of the *obkom*. This was a report to the Central Committee in which the local Party leadership gave assurances that all the workers in Novocherkassk understood the government's policy, and that they would make every effort to fulfil the production plans. The reading was met with laughter from the crowd. This episode bears witness to the distance in consciousness between the Party authorities and the population.

According to Podoloskii, the militia first arrived at the *gorkom* when the demonstration itself was about to disperse. At that point there were only about 1,000 demonstrators left. The soldiers positioned themselves between the *gorkom* building and the crowd, and opened fire against the demonstrators after a single warning shot.

Viktor Valentinovich Kondryashov's eyewitness report confirms the key points in Podoloskii's. In 1962 he was a fifth grade-pupil. Walking in the street on 2 June, he noticed the demonstration and followed it. When the demonstrators reached the *gorkom*, some of them entered the building unhindered in order to engage representatives from the *gorkom* in discussion, but the building was empty. Kondryashov, who had followed the procession, reports that outside on the square could be heard shouts such as: 'How can we continue to live like this?' and 'There is nothing to eat.' He recalls that this made no great impression on him because he was used to hearing such things. Suddenly a column of tanks drove in between the *gorkom* building and the demonstrators, and shortly afterwards a group of soldiers opened fire on the crowd which had followed the tanks. Kondryashov saw no instances of violence or vandalism on the part of the demonstrators.[50]

The lawyer S. Oganosov, who was present on the square in front of the Gorkom on 2 June, reports that there was absolutely no question of rioting; on the contrary, this was a case of peaceful, spontaneous action from a large group of people who were dissatisfied with their situation. After the events he had been the defence lawyer at the trial of a boy who had inadvertently come into the first row of the demonstration; he had merely wanted to see what was happening, but turned up on the KGB agents' photographs and was therefore sentenced to 10 years' imprisonment.[51]

Simultaneously with the events around the *gorkom*'s headquarters, according to the KGB's reports, groups of demonstrators attempted to occupy the KGB and militia buildings. They demanded that the arrested demonstrators be released and attempted to appropriate documents. This led to fighting, in which clubs and knives were brought out. However, there was no mention of any killed or wounded. Finally the authorities succeeded in turning the demonstrators out, and regained control of the buildings.

The latter events are not confirmed by any of the other eyewitnesses. On the other hand they are discussed in detail in Defence Minister Yazov's report on the events to the People's Congress in 1991. He declared that no fewer than 2,975 regular troops were sent to Novocherkassk on 1 June 1962, and that these troops had not only been involved in action at the train factory and the Party headquarters, but had occupied the bank, post office, telegraph, police station, KGB headquarters, prison and electricity works. According to Yazov this occurred because the demonstrators had attempted forcibly to occupy these buildings.[52] Yazov's account of the events implies that it was a more-or-less organized revolutionary uprising, which was, despite everything, hardly the case. His version can be explained only by a desire to justify the heavy-handed intervention of the state.

Even after these dramatic events, which showed very clearly that the authorities did not shrink from using the most violent methods at their disposal, the strikers continued to hold meetings in front of the *gorkom* and the KGB buildings. It was night-time before the soldiers succeeded in dispersing the demonstrators. The following morning, however, on 3 June, around 500 people again gathered in front of the militia headquarters and demanded the immediate release of the demonstrators who had been arrested the day before. According to the report, one of the demonstrators in particular drew the attention of the crowd. This was a woman who, with deep indignation, accused the soldiers of having killed her son the day before, when the latter had climbed up a tree to follow the events. The crowd was deeply affected by this, and tension grew.

The propaganda effort

Already by the morning of 3 June the Party had set in motion an intensive propaganda campaign among the city's residents. The Party attempted, reportedly with a certain success, to convince the population that it was criminals and troublemakers who were behind the demonstration, and to assure them that these people would be quickly tracked down and made to answer for their actions. The propaganda effort culminated in a speech on radio by Kozlov, which was broadcast at 3 p.m. that day on local radio. Thereafter, according to the sources, the city gradually calmed down, although 'evil shouts and threats' could still be heard from a few of the 'most hardened elements'.

Before following the report further, we will look briefly at Kozlov's radio speech, which in many ways clearly illustrates the techniques used by the authorities to quell the unrest. Kozlov (1908–65), who was Secretary of the Central Committee and a member of the Presidium of the Communist Party, had arrived in Novocherkassk on 2 June, together with Mikoyan (1895–1978), Deputy Chairman of the Council of Ministers and likewise a member of the Presidium. The radio speech, broadcast, as already stated, at 3 p.m. on 3 June, could be heard only in the Novocherkassk region.[53] Kozlov was aware that a majority of the workers at the train factory had taken part in the demonstration, and that they had won support from a significant proportion of workers from other factories, as well as from the rest of the population, but this fact was not mentioned in the speech. In his version mention was made only of a small group of trouble-makers and criminal elements, without whose banditry the events would never have gone so far. In fact, nothing in the course of events themselves indicated that there was any question of a consciously planned action; on the contrary, this was a spontaneous protest, which quickly won sympathy and support from a large segment of the population. The rest of the radio speech demonstrates that Kozlov was aware of this, and that it was not enough, therefore, to single out a particular group and prosecute them. The second part of the strategy therefore consisted of an admission that the workers' dissatisfaction was to a certain extent justified together with a partial concession to their demands. Kozlov thus pushed the blame for the events onto individual managers at the train factory and onto the local Party leadership, some of whom were demoted or removed. He took the initiative to remedy the supply situation, so that by 3 June the city's shops, which for a long time had stood virtually empty, were filled with food products and other consumer goods, and he promised to annul the reduction in wages that had been instituted. All this may have helped to create the perception that the central Party leadership was on the side of the workers, and at the same time may have strengthened the first of the Party leadership's tactics, which, as we have seen, was to isolate the trouble-makers, who had led the masses astray and made them doubt the Party's good intentions. This is the probable explanation for the fact that the situation in the city returned to normal relatively quickly. By 4 June normal work had generally been resumed in the town's factories. Of course the ever-increasing number of soldiers on the streets, the curfew, the killing of demonstrators and not least the executions which followed in the wake of the events of 1–4 June must have contributed significantly to subduing the atmosphere in the city.

Kozlov rejected the demand for the price rises to be abolished, and in that connection repeated the argument in the Party press that it was essential for the government to have the means to institute improvements in the agricultural sector. He also rejected, as had the Party press, the possibility of taking more money from industry or defence on the grounds that this would weaken the foundations of socialism and increase the danger of hostile invasion. However, there was an important detail in Kozlov's speech which was not to be found in the

Party press or in Khrushchev's speech to the population on the evening before the price rises were put into effect: namely, a promise that they would only be temporary. This may have been something which Kozlov hit upon himself with the aim of stopping the strikes.

The speech, which as we have seen made concessions in several respects to the strikers' demands, shows that the authorities had allowed themselves to be pushed into negotiations, which in itself represented a distinct break in Soviet tradition. On the other hand, both in the speech and in most of the authorities' other initiatives – the strong military presence, the use of police agents, the shooting of demonstrators and not least the trials after the events – we find a great deal of evidence that the Stalinist tradition still prevailed. Kozlov's speech ended with the following thinly veiled threat: 'Normal order will be restored in the city, no matter what it costs. To work, comrades!'

Podolskii confirms that the unrest continued after the shooting of the demonstrators in front of the *gorkom*. He reports that workers from a number of other factories arrived in trucks, and that around 20,000 people were gathered in the streets. According to the KGB's report, the tension decreased as a result of Kozlov's radio speech, which was broadcast to the city over loudspeakers. Judging from Podolskii's testimony, however, there were more straightforward reasons why the demonstrators dispersed. The number of tanks in the streets had increased throughout the day, and armed soldiers were gradually stationed on the roofs of all the buildings in the centre of the city. He also reports that the city's student dormitories had been occupied and locked so that no one could get out.[54]

On 12 June the Chairman of the KGB, Semichastnyi, was able to write to the Central Committee that everything was back to normal in Novocherkassk.[55] The population had reacted with satisfaction to the improved situation with regard to supplies, and the workers at the train factory had welcomed the new director. On 9 June a group of workers from the factory's foundry, where the strike had originated, applied to the management for permission to work on Sundays to make up for work that had been missed during the strike. The management had responded sympathetically to the initiative, but asked the workers to stay at home and use Sunday for the purpose it was meant for, namely as a day of rest. It was also reported that several workers had gone to the police station to express regret for their actions.

It is difficult to tell whether Semichastnyi exaggerated the positive results of the authorities' intervention. We cannot exclude the possibility that he wished to set himself, his organization and the Party leaders with whom they had co-operated in a positive light. The subsequent court proceedings, which we will presently return to, perhaps testify to the fact that the mood of unrest had not been entirely quieted, and that a further, more straightforward illustration of the authorities' power and ruthlessness was needed.

According to Lieutenant General Matvei Kuzmich Shaposhnikov, who was removed from his post in 1966 and expelled from the Party in 1967, and who in 1962 had been the Deputy Commander of the North Caucasian forces, the events of 1962 could have led to a tragedy of much greater proportions than in fact occurred. In an interview in 1989 he stated that already on 20 May 1962 General I.A. Pliev had received a coded telegram from Khrushchev, via the Defence Minister Malinovskii, saying that he should put his troops in a state of battle-readiness and station them near Novocherkassk.[56] This suggests that even before news came of the price rises, the situation in the city was critical. Shaposhnikov was ordered by Pliev to lead the troops that were to be stationed at the locomotive factory. At the same time it was made clear to him that before the operation began he should report to Kozlov and Mikoyan, who were staying at a military camp outside Novocherkassk. Shaposhnikov relates that he attempted to persuade the latter to give orders that the soldiers and tank forces should not be provided with ammunition. Kozlov dismissed this advice, saying that Pliev had been given the necessary orders. Later he attempted to persuade Pliev and Ivashchenko, who was a member of the Defence Committee, to send a joint telegram with him to Khrushchev at least giving orders that the ammunition be withdrawn. But they did not agree to this. When Shaposhnikov arrived at the factory on 1 June, he gave orders on his own initiative that the ammunition be collected and put into the safekeeping of the Company commander.

At 11 a.m. on 2 June Shaposhnikov and his troops, including a number of tanks, were stationed on the bridge, which the marchers from the factory would have to cross in order to reach the centre of the city. Shaposhnikov, who was in radio contact with his commander-in-chief, Pliev, was able to inform the latter that around 8,000 demonstrators were marching towards the city. He was ordered to stop the demonstration by force, but replied that he would be unable to do so with so many people involved. Pliev then informed him that he would send tank reinforcements, and ordered Shaposhnikov immediately to attack the demonstrators. The latter however did not comply with this order, but replied: 'Comrade Commander, I cannot see before me any opponent who could appropriately be attacked with our tanks.' Whereupon the connection was cut off, and Shaposhnikov let the demonstrators pass. Later General Parovatkin arrived, bringing a written order to employ weapons. It was the latter who, on this basis, later gave orders to open fire on the demonstrators in front of the *gorkom*.

Shaposhnikov's account of events may of course be an attempt to show himself in a good light, but we know that the demonstrators did not meet with armed resistance from the forces that had been stationed by the bridge. If his information is to be believed, it offers interesting evidence that the central authorities, including Khrushchev, were deeply involved in the events, and that they treated the situation with the utmost seriousness.

The legal proceedings

No sooner had the unrest been quelled on 4 June, than the central authorities began planning legal proceedings against the 14 demonstrators who were said to have been the instigators behind the strike and the demonstrations. Altogether 150 people were arrested and put on remand, but in the first instance the authorities concentrated on these 14. The prosecution's statement, which was completed by the middle of July 1962, was signed by no lesser persons than Colonel Shchebetenko, who was the KGB's Chief Prosecutor for especially important cases, Colonel Mayorov, who was the Deputy Chief of the KGB's investigation department, and finally Ivashutin, the Deputy Chairman of the KGB. Eight of the defendants were charged under Paragraphs 77 and 79 of the penal code, and the remaining six under Paragraph 79. Paragraph 79 related to mass riots, but entailed only a prison or camp sentence. Paragraph 77, however, related to 'banditry', for which the maximum penalty was execution. It was assumed by law, however, that this would be applied only in the case of a manifest organization which had planned the action and carried it out with the use of weapons, with the purpose of injuring or killing the party under attack. There was nothing in the course of events, even in the KGB's version thereof, which justified the application of the ultimate penalty. Nevertheless the eight defendants who were charged under Paragraph 77 were all sentenced to death.

It was decided that the trial of the 14 should be conducted openly, and the authorities sought out a location with space for as many spectators as possible. Their choice fell on the soldiers' club in Novocherkassk, where there was room for 600. At the same time it was decided that the case should be covered by local radio, while the newspapers were forbidden to discuss it. The reason for this ban is a matter of conjecture, but it doubtless had to do with the fact that the authorities were still concerned that knowledge of the case should not spread beyond the region. The threat that unrest might spread to other areas of the Soviet Union may have been greater than the propaganda value that could have been derived from the trial, and the deterrent effect it might have. Nor should it be forgotten that the workers had in fact achieved some results with their action, and the consequences, if this information were to reach other areas, were unforeseeable.

There is a good deal of evidence that the educative and deterrent functions of the trial overshadowed all else, including concern about the justice or otherwise of the prosecution's case. The wording of the prosecution statement alone cannot have given the defendants much hope. They were described as a group of criminal and covetous elements, as the organizers of and participants in mass riots and bandit attacks, and as the instigators of pogroms. They appear in other words to have been convicted in advance. Evidence for this can also be seen in the fact that the KGB's central leadership, together with the *gorkom*, had ensured that the trial was thoroughly orchestrated. Before it began, meetings were held at factories in the region, where the authorities sought in advance to make sure that the workers would demand that the 'trouble-makers' be sentenced to the highest penalty. After the trial was over meetings were likewise held in workers' collectives, where, if one is to believe the reports, the verdicts were unanimously approved. According to the reports, efforts were also made to ensure that the Party line was followed at higher education institutions in the city. Professor Zabludin from the Polytechnic Institute is reported to have said at a meeting: 'These are the scum of society, they have committed the gravest crimes, and they must therefore be shot!'[57]

The show trial of the 14 defendants began on 14 August at the soldiers' club in Novocherkassk. The Chairman of the Supreme Council, A.N. Smirnov, and the State Prosecutor A. Kruglov led the proceedings. By the morning of the 14th the club, which could hold 600 people, was already full. The authorities had made sure that around 500 workers attended each court session. In all 4,000 workers managed to be present at the trial, of which 450 were from the motor factory.[58]

The Deputy Chairman of the KGB, Ivashutin, who was present in Novocherkassk for the trial, was able to inform the Central Committee that the trial had had a great educative effect. At the same time it was recorded that workers who had attended the trial had demanded that the hearing be broken off and that the authorities made sure that 'the criminals be executed immediately.' Shakar, a worker, is reported to have said:

'The defendants are a bunch of good-for-nothings, most of whom have previous convictions. There are two parasites who shouted more than anyone else about poor living standards, but they themselves own their own houses and dachas. One of them moreover has a car, and the other a motorbike. Such people should be excluded from society and sentenced to the highest penalty.'[59]

Another worker, Zaitsev, said of one of the defendants: 'This bandit and drunkard should long ago have been hanged, but they are still bothering with him.' There is no doubt that the trial had been orchestrated, and many of those present were no doubt shouting their comments to order. On the other hand we cannot exclude the possibility that the authorities' propaganda had had a certain effect. As we have seen, its aim was to single out a group of workers as organizers and then to present them in the worst possible light. It was claimed that most of them had had previous convictions and that they were simply out to feather their own nest. Finally, the authorities sought to document that the defendants were among the most materially well-to-do citizens in the community.

The show trial lasted six days. According to the KGB's representative on the spot, the evidence fully exposed the defendants and there was thus no doubt of their guilt. Further confirmation of this was found in the fact that only one of the defendants chose to plead not guilty after all the evidence had been heard. Moreover several of the defendants publicly expressed remorse during the trial. Thus the worker Shubaev said: 'I condemn my criminal activities and express my deep regret to the Supreme Council. I realize that it was not innocent people who were shot, but trouble-makers, and that this was fully justified.' [60] The pronouncement of the verdict, which sentenced seven to death by shooting and seven to terms of between 10 and 15 years in labour camp, was followed by lengthy applause from those present in the crowded hall. Shouts could be heard from the hall, such as 'These dogs will have a dog's death!' 'These wicked criminals went against their brothers and fathers. It's right to shoot them!' Although there were numerous instances of similar irregularities in the form of shouts and expressions of disapproval, the court procedure was described in the reports as orderly and disciplined.

Andre Korkach was arrested on 11 June 1962, because the KGB prosecutor Borodin had conducted a series of interrogations, which he claimed showed that Korkach was one of the ringleaders behind the strikes and demonstrations at the beginning of the month.[61] During the trial itself no fewer than 50 witnesses were brought in, and the report fills 500 pages. Only a few witnesses spoke out in Korkach's defence. The shop steward Yurchenko told the prosecutor that Korkach was known as a skilful worker, and that he enjoyed great authority among the employees. At a series of meetings, however, he had expressed the view that the government's price policy was a mistake. On the same occasions he had expressed his puzzlement that even the smallest price rises abroad were always given great press coverage in the Soviet Union, while here prices could be put up by 30 per cent without a critical word in the press. A head of department, Tomilina, claimed that Korkach had said at one meeting:

'They have cheated us for 45 years, and we haven't been allowed to say anything. Now it's too much, they can put me in prison if they want, I'm not going to keep quiet. The Party's and the Soviet government's policy is wrong as far as the workers' material situation goes.'

One of the most significant testimonies came from the Secretary of the factory's Party organization, P. Urban. When directly questioned by the head of the investigation, he replied that Korkach on several occasions had made insulting remarks about the government and the Central Committee. Amongst other things he is reported to have said: 'Khrushchev is fleecing the country.' Korkach admitted under questioning that he had expressed dissatisfaction with the government's policy and with the use of the militia against the strikers. He also said that he had called for solidarity with the strikers, but he denied having taken part in any form of organized resistance or riots. The following exchange of words between the chief interrogator and Korkach demonstrates what a distance in understanding there was between the two:

Interrogator: When did you realize that a group of violent trouble-makers had forced their way into your factory with the aim of disrupting work?
Korkach: At 11 a.m. I realized – not that a group of violent trouble-makers, but a delegation of workers from the train factory had arrived.

Interrogator: Do you admit that your actions amounted to banditry at the train factory and in Novocherkassk?
Korkach: I do not admit that.

Korkach was one of the seven who were condemned to death by shooting and to confiscation of his property. In the verdict it was stated that the sentence was final and could not be appealed against. He nevertheless attempted to appeal, but his appeal was rejected by the Presidium of the Supreme Soviet of Russia.[62]

In 1989 two journalists found a single document in the Party archive in Rostov which should be presented in this connection. The document was a report of a meeting of the Party's City Committee in Novocherkassk on 4 June 1962. Present at the meeting were prominent guests such as the following members of the Presidium of the Central Committee: F.R. Kozlov, A.I. Mikoyan, D.S. Polyanskii and S.P.Pavlov, who was also the Secretary of the Central Committee of the Komsomol. The report contains a number of sharp and condemnatory statements about the strikers, about the demonstrators and about those Party members who, in the view of the speakers, had not sufficiently adhered to the Party line. One interesting reaction to the events is recorded in full. This came from Professor Ovodov of the local technical school, who said: 'I would like to express the wish that the operations against the provocateurs that are in preparation, and which Frol Romanovich Kozlov discussed in his speech, be put into effect as soon as possible.' If this refers to the show trial, we have evidence that the 'trial' had been planned in advance and arranged centrally.[63]

As has already been discussed, the strikers in Novocherkassk did achieve some positive results. The supply of provisions was rapidly improved, and wages readjusted. At a meeting of the Rostov Regional Committee in July the Director of the train factory, B.N. Kurochkin, was expelled from the Party and fired from his post on grounds of poor management of the plant. The leader of the factory's Party section, M.F. Pererushev, was given a severe reprimand and a black mark in the Party book for poor leadership of the section. The same went for the leader of the *obkom* and several other members of the local Party leadership.[64]

The aftermath: the Party tightens control

In July, following the events in Novocherkassk, the authorities took a series of initiatives whose purpose was to prevent similar events occurring in the future. The sources indicate that Novocherkassk had not been an isolated case. It is clear that there had been both a general increase in cases of anti-Soviet activity and individual occurrences of mass unrest.[65] A commission set up by the Central Committee wrote in its report that the troops from the Ministry of the Interior should be strengthened by special reserves which could be mobilized at short notice to defend public buildings, communications centres, banks, prisons and other important targets. In addition special passport regulations should be introduced in a number of southern regions where there was a particularly high concentration of former convicts. Specific mention was made in this connection of the Rostov region, including the cities Novocherkassk, Taganrog and Shakhty. Other cities named were Krasnodar, Rostov-on-Don, Groznyi, Zheleznovodsk, Koslovodsk, Lermontovskii, Mineralnye vody and Pyatigorsk.

In a decree from the Chairman of the KGB, also dated July 1962, attention was drawn to the fact that, even though the population had unanimously backed Party and government policy, there remained certain socially damaging elements which had come under the influence of foreign propaganda, and which with the help of anti-Soviet agitation and the spreading of false rumours sought to sow distrust towards the Party and the government. It was said that they made use of temporary difficulties in the development towards communism to mislead politically unreliable citizens and persuade them to take part in mass unrest. The decree reads:

> In recent years mass disturbances have occurred in some of our cities, accompanied by pogroms against administrative buildings, the destruction of public property, attacks on representatives of authority and other forms of rioting. The instigators of these disturbances were as a rule troublemakers of a criminal type. During these disturbances however certain individuals of hostile disposition rose to the surface and began to engage in violent activities. These included former German collaborators, churchmen and members of sects, who in a number of cases strove to turn spontaneous events in a counter-revolutionary direction.[66]

This decree by the KGB Chairman Semichastnyi contains a wealth of interesting contradictions. How could he on the one hand claim that the population unanimously backed the regime, while on the other noting an increase in anti-Soviet activity, which in some cases took the form of mass unrest and rioting? He claims that there were more-or-less organized groups behind the disturbances, while at the same time refer-ring to their having arisen spontaneously. Referring to criminal trouble-makers as being, as a rule, the instigators of events, he nevertheless reveals that there were cases in which ordinary citizens were involved. These contradictions may be explained by a split in Semichastnyi's con-sciousness, one that was, moreover, characteristic of the whole Party's outlook. The ideological side of his consciousness told him that the Soviet state was a people's state, and that consequently those who were against the regime did not belong to the people. It was illogical and incomprehensible from an ideological point of view that anyone could go against their own welfare. Therefore those involved must be hard-ened criminals or others with a world outlook which was, as far as he was concerned, incomprehensible and inimical: religious believers and members of sects. His experience from Novocherkassk and elsewhere told him that ordinary workers also took part in the riots, and that these were in fact spontaneous demonstrations, but this he was unable, or rather did not dare, to admit. Such an admission would have had unforeseeable consequences for his own position, his organization and the whole regime. For Semichastnyi, and perhaps for the whole Soviet leadership, anti-Soviet activity could be accounted for only by hostile elements, which had to be neutralized.

Semichastnyi could see only one explanation for the increase in anti-Soviet activity, which was that the KGB had, to far too great an extent, ceased taking sufficient care of state security at the country's large fac-tories and mines. Agents and informers were of course stationed at these places, but the investigation of several instances of mass unrest had demonstrated that they had not shown sufficient vigilance. In any case the authorities had not been warned in advance. Certain remarks in the decree betray, however, that there were other problems apart from the KGB agents' lack of vigilance. Thus mention was made of the necessity of ensuring that the agents and informers had the correct beliefs themselves. Only if this was the case could one count on their giving timely warning about suspicious persons or activities.

The KGB chairman ordered his people at all levels to sharpen their vigilance, not just at military industrial complexes, but also at other plants and factories where many people were employed. In this con-nection it was said that even the slightest attempt at anti-Soviet activity must be stopped immediately. Similarly it was decreed that surveillance of students at higher education institutions should be intensified – not least at those places where foreign students were enrolled.

There is a good deal of evidence that the events in Novocherkassk shook the Soviet authorities to a degree that made them resort to the tried and tested methods of control, punishment and fear – in striking contrast to the political course which the Party had not merely proclaimed since the 20th Party congress, but had also sought to put into practice. It was this policy which had given the population the means to come forward and show their discontent. There is no doubt that the Novocherkassk uprising was a dramatic high point, but it was also the culmination of widespread dissatisfaction with the state of affairs in Soviet society.

Exposure of the arbitrary nature of the Party apparatus

In the late 1980s, when the exposure of falsifications in history was already under way in Soviet society, there were individual critical journalists and researchers who began to take an interest in the events in Novocherkassk in 1962, and who wrote about them in the press. Under pressure from these reports, the case was brought before the first Russian People's Congress in 1990 by a group of deputies, among them the then general director of the train factory where the events had begun. In an enquiry addressed to the Minister of Defence Yazov, the Chairman of the KGB, Kryuchkov, the Minister of the Interior, Bakatin, and the Chief State Prosecutor, Sukharev, a request was made for information on who had been responsible for the use of weapons against the demonstrators in Novocherkassk in 1962, and for these persons to be made to answer for their actions. Yazov's brief and laconic reply was published in the newspaper *Literaturnaya Gazeta* on 12 September 1990. He asserted that it was not the task of the Defence Minister to answer the deputies' enquiry about the reasons for the events in Novocherkassk, to make a judgement about the question of guilt, or to rehabilitate any innocent persons who may have been convicted. He justified his answer by saying that the Ministry did not have sufficient material at its disposal to throw light on the questions raised. This did not, however, prevent the minister from implicitly taking a position on these events. By consistently referring to the strikers as 'bandits', 'a mob', and 'trouble-makers' he not only implied the cause of the events, but also identified who was to blame for them. However, the matter did not stop here. A few months later Yazov's declaration was overruled by the Soviet Supreme Court, which rehabilitated those convicted at the show trial. Only in the case of one of those involved, who had kicked in a door at the city police station, was the conviction upheld, but at the same time it was pointed out that this was in no way sufficient grounds for him to have been sentenced to death. It would be difficult to imagine a clearer exposé of the Soviet regime's arbitrary methods.

From this section it can be seen that active resistance to the actions of the political leadership and, more broadly, to the poor living conditions and work conditions were a constant problem for the leadership throughout the rule of Khrushchev. We also saw elements of persuasive political dissent among the frustrated population. Furthermore it was demonstrated that in spite of Khrushchev's declared departure from the means of control used during the Stalin years violence was employed when uncontrolled societal actions took place. If Khrushchev really regretted such actions, as suggested in his talk about the events in Karaganda with his son-in-law, we may have to face the fact that institutional inertia played a bigger role than the political will of the leader.

Conclusion

The foregoing chapters have given us some insight into how society reacted to the Soviet system in the years of Khrushchev's reign. We saw among other things how he encountered the same problem that plagued all the Soviet leaders: how to get the planned economy to function efficiently. The aim of the reforms was to revitalize Soviet society by means of what the leaders perceived as modernization of the relationship between state and people. Fear of the repressive organs of the state, which had been the most significant mobilizing factor under Stalin, would be replaced by social and political security. This, the political leaders believed, would lay the foundation for creating a relationship of trust between state and society, which in turn would give rise to greater public spiritedness and higher morale among workers. Khrushchev's political reforms came as a relief for the Soviet population, and subsequent efforts to tighten up politically and ideologically could not stifle the sense of freedom which had already spread among them. A certain rise in productivity in both industry and agriculture indicates that the population manifested a greater degree of goodwill towards the system and put more of their energy into the state sector. This increased productivity, however, never resulted in an output which kept pace with expectations, it seldom corresponded to the amount invested, and it was invariably transient. Thus ever-more-dazzling promises of more and better food and decent housing were never even close to being realized. When this became apparent to the population, enthusiasm and discipline waned, and – from the regime's point of view – a negative spiral was set in motion.

If Khrushchev's system is analysed from the perspective of high politics – a perspective that, for obvious reasons, tends to dominate the research – his lack of success is explained by the fact that his reforms were not sufficiently radical. Khrushchev, it is argued, came nowhere near truly delegating decision-making and responsibility by establishing a market and a price mechanism; instead, he clung to the basic principles of Stalin's command-economy system, with all its inbuilt contradictions and lack of economic rationality. I do not doubt the validity of this type of explanation, nor that the planned economy itself, even if Soviet citizens had been extremely conscientious and fulfilled the plans to the letter, would ever have been able to measure up to the market economy in terms of economic efficiency. In this study we have, however, moved a few steps down the latter of abstraction and examined how people reacted to the Soviet system as it was administered in those particular years. Focus has been put on various forms of resistance, mainly disobedience, and it has been argued that such behaviour penetrated all layers of Soviet society. Soviet citizens did not behave as the politicians wished, and it was not without reason that thousands were charged with anti-state or anti-Soviet activity. As a matter of fact they remained relatively immune to the propaganda and were charged because they gave their personal economic interests and goals higher priority than those of the *kolkhoz*, the factory or the Party-state. This 'privatization' of the Soviet economy and of Soviet social life as a whole was not unique to Khrushchev's time, but was present both before and after. Stalin sought to crush it through terror and force, Khrushchev and his successors through various versions of the socialist welfare model; but both methods proved equally ineffective.

As we have seen, both Filtzer and Timofeev emphasize that there are limits to how closely an external power can control the individual worker, and argue that the workers, both in Stalin's and in Khrushchev's systems, therefore had a certain degree of control over their own work output. Filtzer sees the spread of this control as resulting from a defect within the system: the planned economy generates a chronic shortage of labour, which makes managers extremely reluctant to intervene in cases where work discipline has been violated; while Timofeev is more inclined to see the phenomenon as an expression of the individual's urge first and foremost to promote his own, private interests. Filtzer allows the possibility that the problem could be solved through a reform of the system that would eliminate the chronic labour shortage. Timofeev's only solution is a revolution: an overthrow of the entire system to bring it into line with a system that can provide the only real incentive to work, that is, a market economy based on private ownership.

Two of the nine stories tell of active resistance against the conditions which Khrushchev's regime imposed on its citizens. One comes from the forced labour camps which, despite Khrushchev's widespread liberalisation, remained a reality in the Soviet system; the other draws on two examples from Soviet factories. These forms of open revolt, however, did also take place before Khrushchev. Martha Craveri has identified a number of uprisings in Stalin's camps,[1] and James Rossman has given a detailed account of the uprising among textile workers in Ivanovo in 1932.[2] The latter has a good deal in common with the uprising in Novocherkassk, but it differs on one decisive point. By all accounts the troops in Ivanovo did not open fire against the demonstrators, as they did under the 'liberal' Khrushchev. This does not quite square with the perception of Stalin's and Khrushchev's regimes as respectively the 'hard' and 'soft' versions of totalitarianism, but it does point to a certain continuity between the two. Doubtless, too, the difference in the authorities' behaviour testifies to the fact that, whereas Stalin did not feel threatened by the events in Ivanovo, Khrushchev probably felt a good deal less secure in his position. As we know, less than two years after the uprising in Novocherkassk his opponents in the political elite ousted him.

The history of the Soviet Union in general, and the nine stories presented here in particular, demonstrate that there are limits to how far the state can break with traditional methods of mobilizing the population, including the labour force. If pressure from the state becomes too great, parts of society will to a greater or lesser extent 'privatize' their economic activities and the rest of their behaviour. Through this kind of insubordination Soviet citizens were able to a certain extent to evade state control, and this in itself contributed to the problems of economic planning.

Although radically improved access to archival sources has revealed evidence of hitherto unknown cases of open resistance against the Soviet regime, and though we will almost certainly discover more such cases in the future, we are unlikely ever to conclude that it was this form of action which led to the eventual collapse of the system. On the contrary, it was the numerous instances of covert, quiet, everyday disobedience, or the overall lack of loyalty towards the regime, among both the highest and the lowest in society, which would in the end completely undermine its very foundations.

This kind of resistance leads us to some extent to question the historical stereotype of the submissive Russian, humbly bowing to the power of the state, almost irrespective of how unreasonably he was treated. This stereotype has gained widespread currency, as is instanced, for example, by a CIA report from 1957 about resistance to the regimes in Eastern Europe and in the Soviet Union. The report maintained that the resistance in the Eastern European countries was significant, but that the people of the Soviet republics, and particularly the Russians, had generally speaking resigned themselves to their circumstances. The explanation, according to the report, lay, on the one hand, in the fact that the East European countries were anchored in Western culture and, on the other, in the Russians' particular cultural background and the 'traditional passivity' which resulted from this.[3] These images, whose contours would later be drawn together in the concept of a psycho-historical 'iron curtain' between the two worlds of the Western (Roman Catholic) and Eastern (Orthodox) Churches, were almost un-assailable until 1991, when Russia finally broke loose and engendered a new interest in its social history.[4]

The so-called gradualists in the ongoing debate about the effects of the reforms in Russia often use the 'particular nature of Russian civil-ization' as an explanation for why the reforms, in their opinion, failed, while the advocates of quick and radical reform have little to say about this special Russian tradition.[5] The present work demonstrates that Russian society was much more than a passive object for the ideology and control emanating from the leadership. The citizens created a 'second society' or under-society, the values of which ran counter to official ideology and finally undermined the regime.

One could say that society increasingly became a burden to Khrushchev and his successors. A steadily increasing number of Soviet citizens either did not want, or were unable, to behave as their leaders wished, and this in the end led to the collapse of the system.

Brezhnev (1964–1981) attempted, through a mixture of repression and his special brand of welfare policies, which were mainly financed by oil revenue, to gain control over society, but he never succeeded fully in doing so. As the extremely over-extended economic model yielded steadily poorer results, and as oil became harder and harder to access and oil prices began to fall, he lost his grip.

Gorbachev took up where Khrushchev had left off and attempted through liberalization to achieve a compromise with society. As we know, this attempt sparked off an overall disintegration of the state which Gorbachev, unlike his predecessors, no longer had the means to halt.

The present book is not intended to present an argument against the conception of the Party state as a totalitarian regime. The fact that under Khrushchev Soviet power began, to a certain extent, to take society into account, together with the existence of various forms of insubordination and resistance – of actions and forms of behaviour, which went against the political leadership – does not undermine this fundamental premise. Full control never became a reality, but the aspirations for such control were there, and that is sufficient to justify characterizing the regime as totalitarian.

The existence of mass criticism in Russian history does not of course mean that a democratic Russia lay just beneath the surface, and was merely waiting for an opportunity to come forth, but it does suggest that there was both diversity within Soviet society and an awareness of the inhumanity and injustice of the system. This may help to explain why the Party-state fell apart so easily in 1991. It is possible that the majority had no clear conception of what they wanted in its place, but they knew what they did not want, and that too is a starting point for change.

Notes

Introduction

1. Martin McCauley, *The Khrushchev Era 1953–1964*, Longman, Harlow, 1996.
   Carl A. Linden, *Khrushchev and the Soviet Leadership 1957–1964*, the Johns Hopkins Press, Baltimore, 1966.
2. A.N. Afinogenov, *Strakh*, 1931, Poughkeepsie, Vassar College, New York, 1934, p. 40.
3. McCauley, *The Khrushchev Era*. p. 35.
4. From George W. Breslauer, *Khrushchev and Brezhnev as Leaders: Building Authority in Soviet Politics*, Allen Unwin, London, 1982, p. 37.
5. Ibid., p. 81.
6. McCauley, *The Khrushchev Era*, p. 30.
7. Breslauer, *Khrushchev and Brezknev*, p. 124.
8. Tatyana Zaslavskaya, 'Doklad o neobkhodimosti bolee uglublennogo izucheniya v SSSR sotsialnogo mekhanizma razvitya ekonomiki' *Materiala zamizdata*, RFE-RL, vypusk 35, 1983.
9. J. Rossman, 'The Teikovo Cotton Workers' Strike of April 1932', in: *Russian Review*, vol. 56, no. 1, 1997.
10. S. Davies, 'Us against Them: Social Identity in Soviet Russia 1934–41', in: *Russian Review*, vol. 56, no. 1, 1997.
11. L.M. Timofeev, 'Institutsionalnaya korruptiya sotsialisticheskoi sistemy', in: Yu. Afanasiev, *Sovetskoe obshchestvo*, t.2, RGGU Moscow, 1997.
12. Ibid.
13. Ibid.
14. G.A. Yavlinskii, Ekonomika Rossii, Nasledstvo i vozmozhnosti, EPIcentr, Moskva, 1995.

1. The Closed Letter

1. Naumov in: N.V. Kovaleva and A.N. Jakovlev (eds), *Molotov, Malenkov, Kaganovitch*, MFD, Moscow, 1998, p. 11.
2. Ibid., p. 13.
3. Ibid., p. 16.
4. Ibid., p. 17.
5. TsKhSD, f. 89, op. 6, d. 2, 'Pis'mo TsK KPSS k partiinym organizatsiyam, Ob usilenii politicheskoi raboty partiinykh organizatsii v massakh i peresechenii vylazok antisovetskikh, vrazhdebnykh elementov, 19/12-1956.'
6. Cited from: TsKhSD, f. 89, op. 6, d. 2, 'Pis'mo TsK KPSS k partiinym organizatsiyam, Ob usilenii politicheskoi raboty partiinykh organizatsii v massakh i peresechenii vylazok antisovetskikh, vrazhdebnykh elementov, 19/12-1956.'
7. TsKhSD, f. 89, op. 45, reel 16, d. 611, Serov to Mikoyan and Suslov.
8. Aleksei Adzubei, *Te desyat let*, Sovetskaya Rossiya, Moscow, 1989.

9. TsKhSD, f. 89, op. 6, d. 5, 'V. Churaev, Zav. otdelom Partiinykh Organov, TsK KPSS po RSFSR, Ob antipartiinykh vystupleniyakh otdelnykh kommunistov na sobraniyakh nekotorykh pervitiinykh partiinykh organizatsii pri obsuzhdenii pis'ma TsK KPSS, Ob usilenii politicheskoi raboty partiinykh organizatsii v massakh i peresechenii vylazok antisovetskikh, vrazhdebnykh elementov, 12/2-1957.'
10. Robert C. Tucker, *The Soviet Political Mind*, Pall Mall Press, London, 1963.
11. TsKhS f. 89, op. 6, d. 6, 'V. Churaev, Zav. otdelom Partiinykh Organov, TsK KPSS po RSFSR, Ob antipartiinykh vystupleniyakh .....'
12. TsKhSD, f. 5, op. 32, d. 77, 'V. Churaev, Zav. otdelom Partiinykh Organov, TsK KPSS po RSFSR, O khode obsuzhdeniya pis'ma TsK KPSS Ob usilenii antisovetskikh, vrazhdebnykh elementov partiinykh organizatsiyakh RSFSR, 9/1-1957.'
13. TsKhSD, f. 5, op. 32, d. 77, N. Kapitonov, sekretar MK KPSS, 'O khode obsuzhdeniya pisma TsK KPSS Ob usilenii politicheskoi raboty partiinykh organizatsii v massakh i peresechenii vylazok antisovetskikh, vrazhdebnykh elementov, 4/1-1957.'
14. TsKhSD, f. 5, op. 32, d. 77, Zam.zav. Ot. Pat. organov TsK KPSS RSFSR V. Tishchenko, 'O khode obsuzhdeniya pisma TsK KPSS, Ob usilenii politicheskoi..., 24/1-1967.'
15. TsKhSD, f. 5, op. 32, d. 77, Kannunikov, sek. obkoma Pskov, 'O khode obsuzhdeniya v pervitiinykh partiinykh organizatsiyakh Pskovskoi oblasti pis'ma TsK KPSS Ob usilenii politicheskoi.., 18/1-57.'
16. TsKhSD, f. 5, op. 32, d. 77, 'Bryansk Obkom, O khode obsuzhdeniya pis'ma TsK KPSS Ob usilenii politicheskoi raboty...., 25/1-1957.'

2. The church and the state

1. M.B. Shkarovskii: 'Poslednyaya ataka na russkuyu pravoslavnuyu tserkov' in: *Rossija XX Vek, Sovetskoe Obshchestvo*, Rossiiskii Gosudarstvennyi Gumanitarnyi Universitet, Moscow, 1997.
2. TsKhSD, f. 5, op. 32, d. 12, 'O pervykh otklikakh trudyashchikhsya na postanovlenie TsK KPSS Ob oshibkakh v provedenii nauchno-ateisticheskoi propagandy sredi naseleniya, 13 nov. 1954.'
3. TsKhSD, f. 5, op. 32, d. 12, 'Ob otklikakh trudyashchikhsya na postanovlenie TsK KPSS Ob oshibkakh v provedenii nauchno-ateisticheskoi propagandy sredi naseleniya, 20 nov. 1954.'
4. See: Leon Trockij, Fragen des Alltagslebens, Berlin, 1923.
5. M.B. Shkarovskii, 'Poslednyaya ataka na russkuyu pravoslavnuyu tserkov.'
6. M.B. Shkarovskii, 'Poslednyaya ataka na russkuyu pravoslavnuyu tserkov.'

3. 'Give us decent homes!'

1. TsKhSD, f. 6, d. 1.742
2. TsKhSD, f. 6, op. 6 film 1.981, d. 1.742.
3. Postanovlenie 12/5-1954, 'O poryadke raspredeleniya zhiloi ploshchadi v. g. Moskve.'

4. TsKhSD, f. 6, op. 6, d. 1.742.
5. TsKhSD, f. 6, op. 6, d. 1.754.
6. TsKhSD, f. 6, op. 6, d. 1.742.
7. TsKhSD, f. 6, op. 6, d. 1.742.
8. TsKhSD, f. 6, op. 6, d. 1.742.
9. TsKhSD, f. 6, op. 6, d. 1.742.
10. TsKhSD, f. 6, op. 6, d. 1.742.
11. TsKhSD, f. 6, op. 6, d. 1.754.
12. TsKhSD, f. 6, op. 6, d. 1.754.
13. TsKhSD, f. 6, op. 6, d. 1.754.

4. Economic disobedience

1. Alec Nove, 'Industry' in: Martin McCauley, *Khrushchev and Khrushchevism*, Macmillan, London, 1987, p. 61
2. Martin McCauley, *The Khrushchev Era 1953–1964*, Longman, London, 1995, p. 93.
3. Robert Conquest, *Russia after Khrushchev*, Praeger, New York and London, 1965.
4. D.Filtzer, 'Labour' in: McCauley, *Khrushchev and Khrushchevism*, p. 118.
5. M. Gardner Clark, 'Soviet Agricultural Policy' in: Harry G. Shaffner, *Soviet Agriculture, An Assessment of Its Contributions to Economic Development*, Praeger, London, 1977, p. 21.
6. Ibid., p. 17.
7. Ibid.
8. Ibid., p. 9.
9. Victor Perlo, 'How Agriculture is Becoming an Advanced Section of Socialist Society' in: Harry G. Shaffner, *Soviet Agriculture*, p. 106 ff.
10. G.A.E. Smith, 'Agriculture' in: Martin McCauley, *Khrushchev and Khrushchevism*, p. 114.
11. TsKhSD, f. 6., o. 6, film 1.978, d. 1.726, 'Reshenie, KPK 23.03.59. O zapiske otvet.kontrolera tov. Vologzhanina S.A. o zatyaske stroitel. pushkovykh obektov i krupnykh ubytakh na. Pen. kompressornom zavode (strogo sekretno).'
12. TsKhSD, f. 6, o. 6, film 1.986, d. 1.798 , 'Min. finansov SSSR, Promyshlennyi bank, Penzenskaya obl. kontora, 28. jan. 1959. V KPK.'
13. TsKhSD, f. 6, o. 6, film 1.986, d. 1.798.
14. TsKhSD, f. 6, o. 6, film 1.986, d. 1.798, 'K otchetu VTsK VLKSM Ob uchastii saratovskoi oblastnoi komsomolskoi organizatsii v razvitii khimicheskoi promyshlennosti.'
15. TsKhSD, f. 6, o- 6, d. 1743, 'Zapiski rabotnikov KPK pri TsK KPSS i materialy proverki o sryve postavok ovoshchei i kartofelya dlya g. Moskvy i pripiskakh k vypolneniyu plana sdachi gosudarstvu selkhoz. produktsii. fev.-mai 1961.'
16. TsKhSD, f. 6, o- 6, d. 1743, 'V KPK O faktakh ochkovtiratelstva i sryve postavok ovoshchei i kartofelya dlya g. Moskvy sovkhozami Moskovskogo ovoshchekartofelevodcheskogo tresta.'
17. TsKhSD, f. 89, d. 6, reel 6, film 1994.
18. Ibid.

19. TsKhSD, f. 89, p. 7, reel 6, film 1994.
20. TsKhSD, f. 89, d. 6, reel 6, film 1994, 'V TsK KPSS, O faktakh pripisok i ochkovtiratelstva v Tyumenskoi oblasti, 26.4.61.'
21. TsKhSD, f. 89, d. 5, reel 6, film. 1994, 'Spravka o rezultatakh proverki zhalob, postupivshikh iz Tatarskoi ASSR, o narushenii printsipa dobrovolnosti pri zakupke skota u naseleniya, ijul' 1962.'
22. TsKhSD f. 89, d. 8, reel 6, film 1994, 'Postanovlenie Byuro TsK KPSS po RSFSR protokol nr. 21 ot 12/9-1962. (Sovershenno sekretno).
23. TsKhSD f. 89, d. 9, 'Byuro TsK KPSS po RSFSR 26/7-1956' (strogo sekretno).
24. TsKhSD f. 89, d. 15, 'Postanovlenie Byuro TsK KPSS po RSFSR i Sov. Min. RSFSR: 'O prodolzhayushcheisya praktike sdachi gosudarstvu neupitannogo i malovesnogo skota mnogimi kolkhozami i sovkhozami. (iyun 1959).'
25. TsKhSD f. 89, perechen 17, d. 21 reel 6, film 1994, 'Zamestitelyu predsedatelya byuro TsK KPSS po RSFSR t. Voronovu G.I., predsedatelyu Soveta Ministrov t. Polyanskomu, D.S. ot starshego kontrolera, Khabarovskoi gruppy, komissii kontrolya soveta Ministrov RSFSR – chlena KPSS s. 1927 goda t. Ustinova V.K.'
26. TsKhSD f. 89, perechen 17, reel 6, film 1994, delo 22, 'Postanovlenie (sovershenno sekretno) Byuro TsK KPSS po RSFSR 1961: 'O izvrashcheniyakh, dopushchennykh v Omskoi oblasti pri provedenii khlenozagotovok v 1960.'
27. TsKhSD f. 89, perechen 17, 'Informatsii o 5 plenume obkoma KPSS omskoi oblasti 22/6-1961.'

5. The 1961 Party programme

1. TsKhSD, f. 586, op. 1, d. 6, 20, 201, 206, 235, 239.
2. TsKhSD, f. 586, op. 1, d. 312.
3. TsKhSD, f. 586, op. 1, d. 312.
4. TsKhSD, f. 586, op. 1, d. 312.
5. TsKhSD, f. 586, op. 1, d. 312.
6. TsKhSD, f. 596, op. 1, d. 2, Scott A. Koch, 'Anti-communist Resistance Potential in the Sino-Soviet Block', in: *CIA Cold War Records, Selected Estimates of the Soviet Union, 1950–1959*, Washington DC, 1993.
7. TsKhSD, f. 596, op. 1, d. 2.
8. TsKhSD, f. 596, op. 1, d. 2.
9. TsKhSD, f. 586, op. 1, d. 235.
10. TsKhSD, f. 586, op. 1, d. 235.
11. TsKhSD, f. 586, op. 1, d. 235.
12. TsKhSD, f. 586, op. 1, d. 235.
13. TsKhSD, f. 586, op. 1, d. 235.
14. TsKhSD, f. 586, op. 1, d. 235.
15. TsKhSD, f. 586, op. 1, d. 235.
16. TsKhSD, f. 586, op. 1, d. 235.
17. TsKhSD, f. 586, op. 1, d. 235.
18. TsKhSD, f. 586, op. 1, d. 235.
19. TsKhSD, f. 586, op. 1, d. 235.
20. TsKhSD, f. 586, op. 1, d. 235.

6. Expulsions from the Party

1. Thomas Rigby, *Communist Party Membership in the USSR 1917–1967*, Princeton University Press, Princeton 1968.
2. Ibid., p. 298.
3. Ibid., 303.
4. Ibid., p. 306.
5. TsKhSD f. 6, op. 6, d. 943, 'Svodki o rassmotrenii personalnykh del kommunistov KPK pri TsK VKP za 1937–1951'.
6. Rigby, *Communist Party Membership*, p. 311.
7. Ibid., p. 313.
8. TsKhSD f. 6, op. 6, d. 943, 'Svodki o rassmotrenii personalnykh del kommunistov KPK pri TsK VKP za 1937–1951'.
9. TsKhSD, f. 6, op. 6, d. 1.077, film 1.944, 'Otchet o rabote KPK pri TsK KPSS za 1957 god aprel 1958'.
10. TsKhSD, f. 6, op. 6, d. 1.005, 'Statesticheskie otchety i svedeniya o rassmotrenii apellyatskii KPK pri TsK KPSS za 1956.'
11. Statements from 1954 to 1961.
12. Rigby, *Communist Party Membership*, p. 312.
13. TsKhSD, f. 6, op. 6, d. 1.697.
14. TsKhSD, f.6, op. 6, d. 1997.
15. TsKhSD, f. 6, op. 6, d. 1.69.
16. TsKhSD, f. 6, op. 6, d. 1.718.
17. TsKhSD, f. 6, op. 6, d. 933.
18. TsKhSD, f. 6, op. 6, d. 939.
19. TsKhSD, f. 6, op. 6, d. 943.
20. TsKhSD, f. 6, op. 6, d. 943.
21. TsKhSD, f. 6, op. 6, d. 943.
22. TsKhSD, f. 6, op. 6, d. 1.642.
23. TsKhSD, f. 6, op. 5, d. 935.
24. TsKhSD, f. 6, op. 5, d. 943.
25. TsKhSD, f. 6, op. 5, d. 941.
26. TsKhSD, f. 6, op. 5, d. 937.
27. TsKhSD, f. 6, op. 5, d. 942.

7. A scientist speaks out

1. Zhores A. Medvedev, *Soviet Science*, Norton & Co., Toronto, 1978, p. 88.
2. Ibid., p. 100.
3. Alan H. Luther (ed.), *Advances in Theoretical Physics. Proceedings of the Landau Birthday Symposium, Copenhagen 1988*. Pergamon, Oxford, 1990.
4. TKhSD, f. 89, opisi 16–18, reel 6, film 1994.

8. Uprisings in the camps

1. A.I. Kokurina, 'Vosstanie v Steplage (mai-iyun' 1954 g.)', *Otechestvennye Arkhivy*, no. 4, Moscow, 1994.
2. Ibid., p. 35.

3. Yurii Orlov, *Sbornik dokumentov obcshchestvennoi gruppy sodeistviya vypolneniyu khelsinkskikh soglashenii*, Moscow, 1981.
4. A. Zimin, *Sotsializm i neostalinizm*, Moscow, 1981.
5. Ludmilla Alekseeva and Valery Chalidze, *Mass Unrest in the USSR*, Report No. 19, Pentagon Library, Washington DC, 1985.
6. Ibid.
7. Ibid.
8. TsKhSD, f. 6, op. 6, d. 1.639, film 1.971, 'Zapiski rabotnikov Komiteta partiinogo kontrolya pri TsK KPSS i materialy proverki o narusheniyakh sots. zakonnosti v Kargapolskom ispravitelno-trudovom lagere MVD SSR Arkhangel'skoi oblast. (t. 1)'.
9. TsKhSD, f. 6, op. 6, d. 1.639, film 1.971, p. 165, 'Obyasnenie ot zaklyuchennogo: Aleksandrova, Alekseya Petrovicha, 1931 goda rozhdeniya, osuzhden po ukazu i st. 148, srok 3 goda i 11 mesyatsev.'
10. TsKhSD, f. 6, op. 6, d. 1.639, film 1.971, 'Nachal'nik Gulaga i. Dolgikh t. Shikryatovu M.F., 30.09.1953 (sov. sek. ekz. 1).'
11. TsKhSD, f. 6. op. 6, d. 1.639 (film 1.971), 'Chlen KPSS parti. bil. no. 3604581 Silantev Roman Ivanovich t. Shkiryatovu M.F. 12/9-1953'.
12. TsKhSD, f. 6. op. 6, d. 1.639 (film 1.971), 'Sergei Nikolayevich Chernov Gulyayevu, KPK, 5/9-1953.'
13. TsKhSD, f. 6. op. 6, d. 1.640 (film 1.972), 'Prikaz ministerstva yustitsii soyuza SSR 30/10-1953 (Sovershenno sekretno): O narushenii zakonnosti v Kargopolskom ITD.'
14. *Otechestvennye Arkhivy*, no. 4, Moskva 1994, dokument 16, 'Vosstanie v Steplage (mai-iyun' 1954 g.)'.
15. Ibid., dok. 14.
16. Ibid., dok. 15.
17. Ibid., dok. 21.
18. Ibid., dok. 27.
19. Ibid., dok. 27.

9. Mass unrest

The sources used from the APRF, 'Arkhiv Prezidenta Rossiiskoi Federatsi' are taken from the collection edited by V.A. Kozlov, Neizvestnaya Rossiya XX-vek, Istoricheskoi nasledie, Moscow, 1993.

1. TsKhSD f. 5, op. 32. d.27, 'O massovykh besporyadakh sredi rabochikh byvshikh stroibatov tresta no. 96 (g. Kemerovo).'
2. TsKhSD f. 5, op. 32. d.27, 'O massovykh besporyadakh sredi rabochikh byvshikh stroibatov tresta no. 96 (g. Kemerovo).'
3. TsKhSD f. 5, op. 32. d.27, 'O massovykh besporyadakh sredi rabochikh byvshikh stroibatov tresta no. 96 (g. Kemerovo).'
4. Much of the information in this paragraph is based on the Russian historian V.S. Lelchuk's article 'Rasstrel v Temirtau', in: Yu. N. Afanasev and V.S. Lelchuk (eds), *Sovetskoe obshchestvo, RRGU*, Moscow, 1997. In addition see: 'O polozhenii del na stroitelstve Karagandinskogo Metalurgicheskogo zavoda, 17/10-1959', TsKhSD, f. 89, op. 6. d. 10.
5. Lelchuk, 'Rasstrel v Temirtau', p. 308.

6. Ibid., p. 320
7. Ibid., p. 325. Khrushchev's statement was recalled by his son-in-law Adzubei in a conversation with the historian Lelchuk.
8. 'O povyshenii zakupochnykh (sdatochnykh) tsen na prikupnyi rogatyi skot, svinei, ovets, ptitsu, maslo zhivotnoi i slivki i roznichnykh tsen na myaso, myasnye produkty i maslo zhivotnoie, 1962.'
9. APRF, f. 3. op. 58, d. 211, l. 130–132, 'Zapiska predsedatelya Komiteta Gosudarstvennoi Bezopasnosti pri Sovete Ministrov SSSR V. E. Semichastnogo Pervomu Sekretaryu TsK KPSS N. S. Khrushchevu', 4/6-1962.
10. APRF, F. 3, op. 58, d. 211, p. 133–137.
11. Semichastnyi on the unrest in 1962.
12. APRF, f. 3, op. 43, d. 115, l. 53–59, 'Iz zapiski Otdela Partiinykh Organov TsK KPSS po Soyuznym respublikam Otdela Partiinykh Organov TsK KPSS po RSFSR v TsK PPSS o rabote partiinykh organizatsii v svyazi s postonovleniem Soveta Ministrov SSSR o povyshenii zakupochnykh i roznichnykh tsen na produkty zhivotnovodstva, 4/6-1962.'
13. Lelchuk, 'Rasstrel v Temirtau', p. 308.
14. Ibid.
15. *Istoricheskii Arkhiv* no. 1 1993, p. 117, 'Informatsiya Predsedatelya KGB pri SM SSSR V.E. Semichastnogo v TsK KPSS o vrazhdebnykh proyavleniyakh v otdelnykh raionakh strany v svyazi s postanovleniem TsK KPSS i SM SSSR ot 31 maya 1962.'
16. APRF, f. 3, op. 58, d. 211, l. 96–97, 'Zapiska predsedatelya Komiteta Gosudarstvennoi Bezopasnosti pri Sovete Ministrov SSSR V.E. Semichastnogo v TsK KPSS', 2/6-1962.
17. APRF, f. 3, op. 58, 'Zapiska predsedatelya Komiteta Gosudarstvennoi Bezopasnosti pri Sovete Ministrov SSSR V.E. Semichastnogo v TsK KPSS', 2/6-1962.
18. APRF, f. 3, op. 43, d. 115, l. 7-13, 'Iz informatsii Otdela Partiinykh Organov Tsk KPSS po RSFSR ob otnoshenii naseleniya k povysheniyu zakupochnykh i roznichnykh tsen na producty zhivotnovodstva', 2/6-1962.
19. APRF, f. 3, op. 58, d. 211, 'Zapiska predsedatelya Komiteta Gosudarstvennoi Bezopasnosti pri Sovete Ministrov SSSR V.E. Semichastnogo Pervomy Sekretaryu TsK KPSS N.S. Khrushchevu, 2/6-1962.'
20. APRF, f. 3, op. 58, d. 211, 'Zapiska predsedatelya Komiteta Gosudarstvennoi Bezopasnosti pri Sovete Ministrov SSSR V.E. Semichastnogo Pervomy Sekretaryu TsK KPSS N.S. Khrushchevu, 2/6-1962.'
21. APRF, f. 3, op. 43, d. 115, l. 7-13, 'Iz informatsii Otdela Partiinykh Organov TsK KPSS po soyuznym respublikam i Otdela Partiinykh Organov TsK KPSS po RSFSR ob otnoshenii naseleniya k povysheniyu zakupochnykh i roznichnykh tsen na produkty zhivotnovodstva', 2/6-1962.
22. *Istoricheskii Arkhiv* no. 1 1993, p. 115, 'Informatsiya predsedatelya KGB pri SM SSSR V.E. Semichastnogo v TsK KPSS o dopolnitelno postupivshikh v KGB pri SM SSSR dannykh o reagirovanii otdelnykh lits na postanovlenie TsK KPSS i SM SSSR ot 31 maya 1962 g.'
23. *Istoricheskii Arkhiv* no. 1 1993, p. 113, 'Informatsiya predsedatelya KGB pri SM SSSR V.E. Semichastnogo v TsK KPSS o dopolnitelno postupivshikh v KGB pri Sm SSSR dannykh o reagirovanii naseleniya na postanovlenie TsK KPSS i SM SSSR ot 31 maya 1962 g.'

24. APRF, f. 3, op. 58, d. 221, l. 89–91, 'Zapiska zamestitelya predsedatelya KGB pri Sovete Ministrov SSSR P.I. Ivashutina v TsK KPSS, 1/6-1962.'
25. APRF, f. 3, op. 58, d. 221, l. 89–91, 'Zapiska zamestitelya predsedatelya KGB pri Sovete Ministrov SSSR P.I. Ivashutina v TsK KPSS, 1/6-1962.'
26. *Istoricheskii Arkhiv* no. 1 1993, p. 113, 'Informatsiya predsedatelya KGB pri SM SSSR V:E: Semichastnogo v TsK KPSS o vrazhdebnykh proyavleniyakh v otdelnykh raionakh strany v svyazi s postanovleniem TsK KPSS i SM SSSR ot 31 maya 1962 g.'
27. APRF, f. 3, op. 58, d. 211, l. 96–97, 'Zapiska predsedatelya Komiteta Gosudarstvennoi Bezopasnosti pri Sovete Ministrov SSSR V.E. Semichastnogo v TsK KPSS, 2/6-1962.'
28. *Istoricheskii Arkhiv* no. 1 1993, p. 115, 'Informatsiya predsedatelya KGB pri SM SSSR V:E: Semichastnogo v TsK KPSS o vrazhdebnykh proyavleniyakh v otdelnykh raionakh strany v svyazi s postanovleniem TsK KPSS i SM SSSR ot 31 maya 1962 g.'
29. APRF, f. 3, op. 58, d. 211, l. 96–97, 'Zapiska predsedatelya Komiteta Gosudarstvennoi Bezopasnosti pri Sovete Ministrov SSSR V.E. Semichastnogo v TsK KPSS, 2/6-1962.'
30. APRF, f. 3, op. 58, d. 211, l. 98–100, 'Zapiska predsedatelya Komiteta Gosudarstvennoi Bezopasnosti pri Sovete Ministrov SSSR V.E. Semichastnogo v TsK KPSS, 2/6-1962.'
31. APRF, f. 3, op. 58, d. 211, l. 92–95, 'Zapiska predsedatelya Komiteta Gosudarstvennoi Bezopasnosti pri Sovete Ministrov SSSR V.E. Semichastnogo v TsK KPSS', 2/6-1962.'
32. APRF, f. 3, op. 43, d. 115, l. 53–59, 'Iz zapiski Otdela Partiinykh Organov TsK KPSS v TsK KPSS o rabote partiinykh organizatsii v svyazi s postanovleniem Soveta Ministratov SSSR o povyshenkii zakupochnykh i roznichnykh tsen na produkty zhivotnovodstva, 4/6-1962.'
33. APRF, f. 3, op. 58, d. 211, l. 96–7, 'Zapiska predsedatelya Komiteta Gosudarstvennoi Bezopasnosti pri Sovete Ministrov SSSR V.E. Semichastnogo v TsK KPSS', 2/6-1962.'
34. APRF, f. 3, op. 58, d. 211, l. 96–7, 'Zapiska predsedatelya Komiteta Gosudarstvennoi Bezopasnosti pri Sovete Ministrov SSSR V.E. Semichastnogo v TsK KPSS', 2/6-1962.'
35. APRF, f. 3, op. 43, d. 115, l. 53–9, 'Iz zapiski Otdela Partiinykh Organov TsK KPSS po Soyuznym respublikam Otdela Partiinykh Organov TsK KPSS po RSFSR v TsK KPSS o rabote partiinykh organizatsii v svyazi s postanovleniem Soveta Ministrov SSSR o povyshenii zakupochnykh i roznichnykh tsen na produkty zhivotnovodstva', 4/6-1962.'
36. APRF, f. 3, op. 58, d. 211, l. 96–7, 'Zapiska predsedatelya Komiteta Gosudarstvennoi Bezopasnosti pri Sovete Ministrov SSSR V.E. Semichastnogo v TsK KPSS, 2/6-1962.'
37. APRF, f. 3, op. 58, d. 211, l. 96–7, 'Zapiska predsedatelya Komiteta Gosudarstvennoi Bezopasnosti pri Sovete Ministrov SSSR V.E. Semichastnogo v TsK KPSS, 2/6-1962.'
38. APRF, f. 3, op. 58, d. 221, l. 89–1, 'Zapiska zamestitelya predsedatelya KGB P.I. Ivashutina v. TsK KPSS, 1/6-1962.'
39. APRF, f. 3, op. 43, d. 115.

40. Jurilj Bespalov, Valerii Konovalov, 'Novocherkassk, 1962', in: L.A. Kirshner, *Svet i teni – Velikogo deshatiletiya, N.S. Khrushchev i ego vremja*, Lenizdat, Moscow, 1989.
41. It was the Oblast paper 'Molot' and the town paper 'Znamya kommuny'. Vladimir Fomin, *Literaturnaya Gazeta*, 27/4-1991.
42. Komsomolskaya *Pravda*, 27/4-1991.
43. Vladimir Fomin, *Literaturnaya Gazeta*, 27/4-1991.
44. *Komsomolskaya Pravda*, 27/4-1991.
45. O. Volkov, *Komsomolskaya Pravda*, 27/4-1991.
46. *Istoricheskii Arkhiv*, 1, 1993, p. 122.
47. Bespalov and Konovalov, Novocherkassk, 1989.
48. S. Podolskii, 'Ya byl ochevidtsem tragedii', *Literaturnaya Gazeta*, 31/10-1990.
49. Ibid.
50. *Literaturnaya Gazeta*, 21/6-1989.
51. *Komsomolskaya Pravda*, 2/6-198.
52. *Literaturnaya Gazeta*, 12/9-199.
53. F.P. Kozlov on the local radio 3/7-1962.
54. S. Podolskii, 'Ya byl ochevidtsem tragedii', *Literaturnaya Gazeta*, 31/10-1990.
55. *Istoricheskii Arkhiv* 1, 1993, p. 129.
56. *Literaturnaya Gazeta*, 21/6-1989.
57. *Istoricheskii Arkhiv* 2, 1992, p. 172.
58. *Istoricheskii Arkhiv* 2, 1992, p. 175.
59. *Istoricheskii Arkhiv* 2, 1992, p. 172.
60. Ibid.
61. Irina Kruglyanskaya, *Izvestiya*, 30/3-1991.
62. Irina Kruglyanskaya, *Izvestiya*, 30/3-1991.
63. *Literaturnaya Gazeta*, 21/6-1989.
64. *Istoricheskii Arkhiv* 2, 1992, p. 175.
65. *Istoricheskii Arkhiv*, 1, 1993, p. 56.
66. *Istoricheskii Arkhiv*, 2, 1993, p. 65.

Conclusion

1. Martha Craveri, Unpublished PhD dissertation from European University Institute, Florence, Italy, 2001.
2. James Rossman, 'The Teikovo Cotton Workers' Strike of April 1932', *Russian Review*, vol. 56, no. 1, 1997.
3. Scott A. Koch, 'Anti-communist Resistance Potential in the Sino-Soviet Block', in: *CIA Cold War Records, Selected Estimates of the Soviet Union, 1950–1959*, Washington DC, 1993.
4. Kristian Gerner, Stefan Hedlund and Niclas Sundstrom, *Hjaernridon: Det Europeiska Projektet och det Gåtfulla Ryssland,* Fischer & Co., Stockholm, 1995.
5. Stefan Hedlund and Niclas Sundstroem, *Rysslands ekonomiska reformer*, SNS, Stockholm, 1996.

Bibliography

Adzubei, Aleksei, *Te desyat let*, Sovetskaya rossiya, Moscow 1989.
Afanasev, Yu. N. (ed.), *Sovetskoe obshchestvo*, RGGU, Moscow 1997.
Afinogenov, A.N., *Strakh*, 1931, Poughkeepsie, Vassar College, USA, 1934.
Akshutin, Yurii V., *XX-s'ezd KPSS: Novatsii i dogmy*, Politicheskaya literatura, Moscow 1991.
Alekseeva, Ludmila, Valery Chalidze, *Mass Unrest in the USSR*, Report No. 19, Pentagon Library, Washington DC, 1985.
Boffa, Giuseppe, *Inside the Khrushchev Era*, Marzani/Munsell, New York, 1959.
Breslauer, George W., *Khrushchev and Brezhnev as Leaders: Building Authority in Soviet Politics*, George Allen and Unwin, London, 1982.
Brumberg, Abraham (ed.), *Russia Under Khrushchev*, Praeger, New York, 1962.
Burlatskii, Fedor, *Vozhdi i sovetiki. O Khrushcheve, Andropove i ne tolko o nikh....*, Politicheskaya literatura, Moscow, 1990.
Bushnell, John, 'The New Soviet Man Turns Pessimist', *Survey*, v. 24, no. 2, London 1979.
CIA Cold War Records, Selected Estimates of the Soviet Union, 1950–1959, Washington DC, 1993.
Conquest, Robert, *Power and Policy in the USSR*, Macmillan, London, 1961.
Conquest, Robert, *Russia After Khrushchev*, Praeger, New York and London, 1965.
Crummey, Robert (ed.), *Reform in Russia and the USSR: Past and Prospects*, University of Illinois Press, Chicago, 1989.
S. Davies, 'Us against Them: Social Identity in Soviet Russia 1934–41', *Russian Review*, vol. 56, no. 1, 1997.
Filtzer, Donald, *Soviet Workers and De-Stalinization: the Consolidation of the Modern System of Soviet Production Relations, 1953–1964*, Cambridge University Press, Cambridge, 1992.
Vladimir Fomin, *Literaturnaya Gazeta*, 27/4-1991.
Gerner, K., S. Hedlund and N. Sundstrøm, *Det Europæiske projektet og det gåtfulla Ryssland*, Fischer og Co., Stockholm, 1995.
Hahn, Werner, *The Politics of Soviet Agriculture, 1960–1970*, The Johns Hopkins University Press, Baltimore, 1972.
Isotricheskii Arkhiv, no. 2, 1992, no. 1, 1993, no. 2, 1993.
Izvestiya, 20 March 1991
Katz, Abraham, *The Politics of Economic Reform in the Soviet Union*, Praeger, New York, 1972.
Khrushchev, N.S. (1894–1971). *Materialy nauchnoi konferentsii prosveshchennoi 100-letiju so dnya rozhdeniya N. S. Khrushcheva*, Gorbachev Fond, Rossiiskii Gosudarstvennyi Gumanitarnyi Universitet, Moscow, 1994.
Kirshner, L.A., *Svet i teni – velikogo desyatiletiya, N.S. Khrushchev i ego vremya*, Lenizdat, Moscow, 1989.
Komsomolskaya pravda, 27 April 1991.
Kozlov, V.A., *Neizvestnaya Rossiya XX veka*, Istoricheskoie nasledie, Moscow 1993.

Kovaleva, N.V. and A.N. Jakovlev (eds), *Molotov, Malenkov, Kaganovitch*, MFD, Moskva, 1998.

Lakshin, Vladimir, *Novyi mir vo vremena Khrushcheva. Dnevnik i poputnoe 1953–1964*, Knizhnaya Palata, Moscow 1991.

Literaturnaya Gazeta, 21 June 1989, 31 October 1990, 12 September 1990.

Linden, Carl, *Khrushchev and the Soviet Leadership 1957–1964*. Johns Hopkins Press, Baltimore, 1966.

Luther, Alan H. (ed.), *Khrushchev and Khrushchevism*, Macmillan, London, 1987.

McCauley, Martin, *The Khrushchev Era 1953–1964*, Longman, Harlow, 1996.

McCauley, Martin, *Khrushchev and Khrushchevism*, Macmillan, London, 1987.

Medvedev, Roy, *Khrushchev*, Anchor Press, New York, 1983.

Medvedev, Zhores, *Soviet Science,* Norton and Co., Toronto, 1978.

Milyukov, P.N., *Russia and its Crisis*, Collier Macmillan, London, 1969.

Orlov, Yurii, *Sbornik dokumentov obshchestvennoi gruppy sodeistviya vypolneniyu khelsinskikh soglashenii*, Moscow, 1981.

Obcshchestvennye Arkhivy, no. 1, no. 4, Moscow 1994.

Pipes, Richard, *The Russian Intelligentsia*, Columbia University Press, New York, 1961.

Ploss, Sidney I., *Conflict and Decision-Making in Soviet Russia: a Case Study of Agricultural Policy 1953–1963*, Princeton University Press, Princeton, 1965.

Rigby, Thomas, *Communist Party Membership in the USSR 1917–1967*, Princeton University Press, Princeton, 1968.

Rossman, J., 'The Teikovo Cotton Workers' Strike of April 1932', *Russian Review*, vol. 56, no. 1, 1997.

Rothberg, Abraham, *The Heirs of Stalin: Dissidence and the Soviet Regime 1953–1970*, Cornell University Press, London, 1972.

The *Russian Review*, v. 56, no. 1, 1997.

Schapiro, Leonard (ed.), *The USSR and the Future. An Analysis of the New Program of the CPSU*, Praeger, New York and London, 1963.

Scott A. Koch, 'Anti-communist Resistance Potential in the Sino-Soviet Block', in: *CIA Cold War Records: Selected Estimates of the Soviet Union, 1950–1959*, Washington DC, 1993.

Shaffer, Harry G., *Soviet Agriculture: An Assessment of Its Contributions to Economic Development*, Praeger, New York, 1977.

Shatz, Marshall S., *Soviet Dissent in the USSR: Novyi mir and the Soviet Regime*, Praeger, New York, 1982.

Scott A. Koch, 'Anti-communist Resistance Potential in the Sino-Soviet Block', in: *CIA Cold War Records: Selected Estimates of the Soviet Union, 1950–1959*, Washington DC, 1993.

M.B. Shkarovskii: 'Poslednyaya ataka na russkuyu pravoslavnuyu tserkov' in *Rossija XX Vek, Sovetskoe Obshchestvo*, Rossiiskii Gosudarstvennyi Gumanitarnyi Universitet, Moscow, 1999.

Talbott, Strobe, *Khrushchev Remembers*, Boston, 1970, 1974.

Timofeev, L.M., 'Institutsionalnaya korruptsiya sotsialisticheskoi sistemy', in: Yu. Afanasiev, *Sovetskoe obshchestro*, t. 2, RGGU, Moscow, 1997.

Tucker, Robert C., *The Soviet Political Mind*, Pall Mall Press, London, 1963.

Tucker, Robert C., *Political Culture and Leadership in Soviet Russia: From Lenin to Gorbachev*, Wheatsheaf Books Ltd., Brighton, 1987.

Vucinich, Alexander, *Empire of Knowledge*, University of California Press, Berkeley, 1984.

Zaslavskaya Tatyana, 'Doklad o neobkhodimosti bolee uglublennogo izucheniya v SSSR sotsialnogo mekhanizma razvitya ekonomiki', *Materiala zamizdata*, *RFE-RL*, vypusk 35, 1983.

G.A. Yavlinskii, Ekonomika Rossii, Nasledstvo i vozmozhnosti, EPIcentr, Moscow, 1995.

Zimin, A., *Sotsializm i neostalinizm*, Moscow 1981.

Archive Materials

Tsentralnoe Khranenie Sovremennoi Dokumentatsii (TsKhSD)
Fondy: 89, 5, 6, 586.
Arkhiv Presidenta Rossiiskoi Federatsii (APRF) (Printed in *Neizvestnaya Rossiya XX-veka*).

Index